JANUARY 2023

AN ANTHOLOGY OF ARTICLES

BRAIN BOOSTER ARTICLES

Contents

Preface

"Start writing, no matter what. The water does not flow until the faucet is turned on".

- Louis L'Amour

This book is a bouquet of articles contributed by students, professors and academicians. Hundreds of students and professors are contributing their work to Brain Booster Articles, we are here to provide ample information about Law and Contemporary issues. Our aim is to provide a platform for today's generation to express their views and ideas on law and contemporary law.

CHAPTER ONE

25th AMENDMENT ACT, 1971

Author: Anil kumar Raj Purohit, III year of B.com.,LL.B.(Hons.) from Vels University

INTRODUCTION

In 25th amendment the parliament curtailed the right to property which was given as the fundamental right under article 19(1) (f), and permitted the government to acquire the private property for public use. And also added that the payment of compensation should be determined by the parliament and not by the court of law. In 1970, the Supreme Court, in its judgement on RustomCavasjee Cooper v. Union Of India, which is basically also known as the Bank Nationalization case, held that the Constitution guarantees the right to compensation which is provided under article 31, to pay the adequate compensation to for the private property which is acquired or requisitioned by government for the public purpose. And the court held that the law for requisitioned of property should fulfil the requirement in article 19(1)(f). This amendment was introduced to overcome the restriction imposed on government by its ruling. Basically article 31 of the constitution as it stands that no law providing for the compulsory acquisition of property which either fixes the amount of compensation or specifies the principle on which the compensation is to be determined and given shall be called in any court of law in the ground that the compensation provided is not adequate. Therefore Supreme Court also uphold the constitutional right, right to compensation.

REASON FOR AMENDMENT

There are two main reason for the amendment, they are

1. Amended the article 31

2. Inserted article 31C

Amended the article 31: According to the Parliament,right to compensationwas creating a disturbance in acquiring the private property for public purpose. So as per the 24th amendment parliament re-established there power to amend any part of the constitution. Taking the power to amend the constitution parliament amended the article 31 as article 31 gives the right to adequate compensation for the acquisition or requisition of the private property for public purpose.And owners of the property use to file a suit of adequate compensation in court. And in 1970 after the Supreme Court judgement in RC cooper Vs Union of India decided that constitution guarantees right to compensation.And thereafter parliament amended the article 31 by replacing and amending the word "compensation" to "amount" of the property acquired or requisitioned. Further they also added that the compensation will be provided as per the principles which is given in law and no such law shall be questioned in any court on the grounds of adequate compensation or the whole part or some amount of otherwise given in cash.

Inserted Article 31 C: Saving of laws giving effect to certain directive principle. Notwithstanding anything contained in article 13, no law giving effect to the policy of the State towards securing the principles specified in clause (b) or clause (c) of article 39 shall be deemed to be void on the ground that it is inconsistent with, or takes away or abridges any of the rights conferred by article 14, article 19 or article 31; and no law containing a declaration that it is for giving effect to such policy shall be called in question in any court on the ground that it does not give effect to such policy.

Provided that where such law is made by the Legislature of a State, the provisions of this article shall not apply thereto unless such law, having been reserved for the consideration of the President, has received his assent.

NOTE: In the year 1969 Indira Gandhi government nationalized 14 private banks, and passed a legislation to run this effect.RustomCavasjee cooper one of the shareholder in one of this bank have challenged this legislation before Supreme Court.He argued that the legislation did not give him adequate compensation, therefore violating his fundamental right to property under Article 31, and freedom to carry on a business under Article 19(1)(g). The Court agreed with Cooper and passed a judgment striking down the relevant portion of the legislation. This made Parliament to pass the 25th Amendment to overturn the decision in R.C. Cooper.

PROPOSAL AND ACCEPTANCE OF AMENDMENT

The 25th amendment 1971, was introduced in the Lok Sabha by H.R Gokhale who was the Law and Justice Minister of India. It was introduced on 28July 1971. As the bill proposed the following:

1. To replace the word in article 31(2) the word 'compensation' for the acquisition of the property to 'amount'. And also stated that amount could be paid otherwise than cash.

2. Clause (2B) was inserted after clause (2A) which stated that the article 19(1) (f) shall not be applicable to law relating to acquisition of property for the public purpose.

3. The bill also introduced article 31C, mentioning any law passed to give effect to directive principle in article 39(b) and 39(c) and also made that such law could not be challenged in any court of law for violating fundamental rights 14, 19, and 31.

The bill was considered by loksabha on 30 November and 1 December 1971. The bill was passed by loksabha (in favour 353 and against 20) on 1 December and 8 December, 1971 respectively. On 20th April 1972 the bill received for assent of PresidentVarahagiri V. Giri and also came into force on the same day. The Prime Minister Indira Gandhi claimed that it is not her or party's intention to weaker the judiciary. And further she stated that 'the judiciary must not take over the parliament'.

AFTERMATH

The 25thamendment was a measure taken by Indira Gandhi to increase the power of parliament. With 24th amendment, 25th amendment was followed by several constitutional amendment and designed to lessen the power of judiciary and enhance the power of parliament. Such amendment are made to priorities the directive principle of state policy over fundamental right. As well as article 31C also mentioned that article 39(b) and (c) would not be open to judicial review.

Short note on kesavanandabharti Vs state of kerala

I have added this case also because in this case 25th amendment was also challenged and made some changes in 25th amendment.

Kesavanandabharati moved to Supreme Court under article 32 for infringing his rights which were article 25, 26, 14, 19 and 31. During this case constitutional validity of 25th amendment was challenged. The Supreme Court in its judgement held that parliament cannot the basic fundamental rights which is now also known as basic structure of constitution. Now after that parliament have power to amend the rest fundamental rights but cannot basic structure. There after Supreme Court struck down the second part of the 25th amendment.

Note: Eventually after the 44th amendment article 31 was repealed and was added in article 300A as constitutional right.

<u>SUMMARY</u>

In this article we have learnt about the why, how, and when the 25th amendment was introduced. As this amendment was to overcome the issues which were was interrupting the government when they acquire or requisite property for public purpose. And the owner of the property use to file a suit of non-adequate compensastion. And this led the issues for the government which should be resolved. Considering this parliament introduced 25th amendment in 1971 and also added some circumstance which were infringing the fundamental rights. Like people cannot ask for judicial review and cannot challenge in any court of law. As this amendment increased the power of the present ruling government and the parliament but in Supreme Court in its judgement of kesavanandabharati Vs state of kerala decided that basic structure of constitution cannot be amended.

<u>REFERENCE</u>
1. V.N Shukla: Constitution of India
2. J.N Pandey: Constitution of India
3. Smriti Roy: Constitutional law
4. Law commission report: law committee
5. Legislative.gov: Web page

CHAPTER TWO

IMPACT OF DOMESTIC VIOLENCE ON CHILDREN IN INDIA: A SOCIO-LEGAL APPROACH

Author: Lina Parvin, III year of B.A.,LL.B.(Hons.) from Indian Institute of Legal Studies, Dagapur, West Bengal

Co-author: Soham Kundu, III year of B.A.,LL.B.(Hons.) from Indian Institute of Legal Studies, Dagapur, West Bengal

ABSTRACT

Domestic violence is undeniably a social issue and many studies show that most women or wives are a victim of this social menace and are affected. However, it affects the family as a whole, especially, the children. Children are the talented, young minds of a developing nation, who are also a victim or witnesses of domestic violence. Domestic violence affects a child just like the mother, it leaves them vulnerable to anger, anxiety, fear, and depression and also changes the mindset of that young person. The main objective of this paper is to understand the severity of this issue, understand the grievous impact of domestic violence on children in India, understand the grass-root level problems, study the role of legal aspects in this regard, and suggest solutions this problem. This paper is an attempt to give a comprehensive idea of the Impact of domestic violence on children, particularly in various regions of India, and the prevalent solutions to overcome this issue. To complete this paper a doctrinal way of study has been used. The authors have gone through various books and articles and accessed various websites related to this topic.

Keywords: Children, Domestic Violence, Impact, Socio-Legal approach, India.

INTRODUCTION

Domestic Violence or abuse can be simplified as the pattern of various forms of abuse used by one to dominate the other. The severity of domestic violence is an issue that is much wider than the term itself. Mostly it is said that women are the victims of domestic violence or abuse but the whole family is affected by one's dominance over the other.A child being a witness of domestic violence or in cases, a victim of such violence affects the whole childhood of that child. It's not just the mothers who are victimized but the children are equally victimized in situations like these. In India, the effect of domestic violence and children being the witness is still normalized which shows the mindset of each person and also how the child will turn out to be in the mere future. There are many other cases where children witness such violence which results in fear, anxiety, and depression in the adolescence age.

DOMESTIC VIOLENCE

Domestic abuse as stated is simply the abuse that shows the dominance of one over others, in a majority of the cases. Reasons can be poverty, use of substances, single parenthood, divorce, shelter placement, or simply the dominating of one party over the house[1].

TYPES OF DOMESTIC VIOLENCE

There are many types of domestic abuse:

Physical Abuse: The common form of abuse that is practiced in India, includes voluntarily causing hurt or grievous hurt with or without a weapon. The reasons behind this form are either to show the dominating position or in want of dowry, etc.

Sexual Abuse: Sexual Abuse as defined in the Domestic Violence Act,2005, says that the form of abuse that humiliates the dignity of a woman. Sexual Abuse is said to take place when one without their willful consent is forced into sexual activity or intercourse. The reason behind such form of abuse is "to control the woman" and reproduction.

Emotional Abuse: emotional or psychological abuse is said to happen when one usesothers' character, and exploits. It is mostly gender inequality abuse. It can happen in the form of jokes, brainwashing, and manipulation. Any form which causes emotional disempower is abuse.

Economic Abuse: Controlling the expenditures of one or not allowing them to spend at all. In many cases, the woman who is housewives have to depend on financial aid from their husband and that's where the husband uses such vulnerability to control those expenses.

Neglect: When one is neglected, that is they are completely being ignored like they do notexist. Neglect is one form of abuse that overlaps with the other mentioned forms of abuse.

In all these types of violence, the victim, although are the woman, wives, and mothers but children, are the silent group of domestic violence, whether a witness or a victim themselves[2].

CAUSES BEHIND DOMESTIC VIOLENCE

To understand the depth of such impact on children, it is important to understand the reason behind domestic violence. The reasons are:

A patriarchal society: In the 21st century, the societal norms still lie, the patriarchal mindset of people that women need no rights, no rights should be provided and that they are inferior to men, and if they try to raise their voices then using violence is the only way to stop them. The women according to the so-called belief have no opinion of their own, if they have any opinion then they are abused in various forms.

Economic Instability: India is a developing nation that still lives in poverty. It is also to be noted that the impact of COVID-19 had a huge impact on this economical condition relating to an individual and cases of domestic violence and divorce were at large. The complaints of domestic violence snowballed as 1477 complaints were registered between March 25 and May 31 in 2020 (68 days) which was more than the complaints received between March and May in the previous 10 years.

In want of dowry: one of the most famous reasons, in India domestic violence arises in want of dowry. Dowry death has been a major concern because of the majority grievousness in this case. It is not just the husband who is the attacker but it might also be the relative of the husband who abuses the wife in want of dowry.

Substance Abuse:Alcohol and drug abuse are also something that can be commonly found as a reason or cause behind domestic violence. Even children can sometimes be a victim of this domestic violence.

Psychological Disorder: A person of an unsound mind, the one who losses control due to a psychological illness can be one of the reasonsfor domestic violence.

Past Experience: A child who has seen, who has been a witness to domestic violence, growing up to be just like the father as he thinks it is important to show masculinity or to show women as inferior. This kind of behavior or mindset is a result of childhood experience, where he thinks, or what he is taught that it is something normal[3].

IMPACT ON CHILDREN

WHO IS A CHILD?

Article 1 of the convention on the right of children, which lays down who is a child expresses that a child is a person who is under the age of 18 years[4].

Domestic Violence on a Child

Domestic abuse, as mentioned is something where not only the mother but the children are equally the victim of such violence. It might result in mental traumas, like depression, and anxiety[5]. Experience changes everything. Where one lives in fear, another sets the fear in the future. Domestic Violence and child protection is a complex area. A child is someone who needs a safe and secure environment and an openness of mind so that he can grow up well, but in such an environment even where that child is continuously witnessing domestic violence, it results in developmental problems, behavioral problems, and they carry these traumas to the adulthood also. This can even use the child serious health diseases and can developmentally condition like depression which are most common among children. COVID-19 has seen a surge in domestic violence and thus the child is a witness or victim who has been through a lot, as he has nowhere to go and has caused many troubles[6]. They even indulge themselves in substances usages which destroy the future of that child. So, they must be some serious action taken to measure the safeguard of children as they are the neglected persons in this domestic violence.

LEGAL PROVISION

Children who are a victim of domestic violence must have a legal safeguard. This legal provision will analyze the protection of children and safeguarding their rights:

Constitution of India[7]

It is well known that the constitution is the main law of the land, and all laws, and statutes come under the purview of this act. There are many provisions relating to the protection of children that including Article 21A, fundamental rights that ensure free education for children aging from 6 to 14 years. The right to be protected from being abused under Article 39(e) although ensures the right for children but it is the state who needs to look upon this as this is a directive principle of state policy. Other directive principal rights include the right to be in an equal opportunity under article 39(f) and facilities to develop in a healthy and safe environment and the right to early childhood care under article 45. Most of the rights of children are included under DPSP and it is the state who looks upon this non-justiciable right.

Juvenile Justice Act, 2000[8]

The act has provided an establishment for the child welfare committee for disposing of the matters of the child conflict with laws. The act provides for the care, protection, rehabilitation, and development of children. Not only that, but the act also enforces the establishment of observational homes for temporary reception, care, protection, and shelter homes for the children who require support.

Protection of Women from Domestic Violence Act, 2005[9]

The act restricts the practice of domestic violence which is common practice in Indian households. The act includes all women who can be protected from Domestic Violence. The protection of children has been overlooked in this act. Although women are the victims, it is the children who are equally the sufferer of domestic violence.

Others

The commission for protection of the Child Rights Act, 2005[10], where the national commission for the protection of child rights was established in 2007. The commission works under the ministry of women and child development. The commission works to ensure that all the laws, policies, and programsalign with child rights. It works on the district level, state level, and block levels taking in ordinances with child care and child rights[11].

IMPACT OF COVID-19

Since the pandemic has stayed, the crisis has risen a lot. Society is still healing or trying to heal from the pandemic and fighting. Since the pandemic, even the cases of domestic violence have risen, a lot, like in India, the total complaints from women rose from 116 in the first week of March, to 257 in the final week of March[12].Similarly, complaints relating to the "right to live with dignity" started rising from 35 cases to 77 cases[13]. Such cases could pertain to discrimination based on gender, class, or caste, or all three of them combined. If that is the case for women, then it will be hard to distinguish the situation in which the children have suffered. The children who cannot speak to anyone, and who are helpless have been consideredto be through a lot more than anyone.

A young mind especially when seeing a father domestically abusing his mother, leaves a mental trauma that haunts forever, and in many cases also, the children are the victims too of such violence.

CONCLUSION

Many children exposed to violence in the homeare also victims of domestic abuse. Children who witness and are a victim of domestic violence are at a greater and more serious risk not only for a short period but for a long period. Parents' being violent in their household is the destruction to the child's future. Children may have difficulty falling asleep, which in the teenage years can convert into insomnia, a disease that is most common among adolescent childrennowadays. They show signs of terror, signs of being frightened, they hide to stop witnessing this crime. They may feel guilty as they think that they are the reason for this happening[14]. They are happy to be left alone, they become shy to share any of these details. They later may use substances[15] to calm themselves. That's what happens when the child has been neglected since childhood. A child can recover from this incident. However, it needs a tremendous amount of work to heal the child. There should be rehabilitation centers, with a more victim-centric approach, where they could help a child be settled, be comforted so that they can be healed. The workers must be trained in treating these children making them feel a safe environment. Teachers who arethe frontliner must help children by spreading awareness, making the children be comforted, and then finally handing that child over to Non-Governmental Organizations working for the rights of children. There must be a well and adequate system of foster care, and for that, a commission must be set up, that can fight for these children'srights, and can send children to foster care with proper evaluation of parents, so that it ensures the safe environment of that child, and also later be adopted.

Domestic violence, impact children on a large scale. Being a victim of domestic violence takes a lot from that child, as a whole childhood. That child could never live the life same as again. So, it is important to understand the grievousness of such an impact on a child and serious steps must be taken to ensure the safeguard of Children.

CHAPTER THREE

ASSESSING DEATH PENALTY AS A LEGAL POLICY CONCERN IN INDIA

Author: Kavya Srinivasan, I year of LL.B. from University of Glasgow

Punishment has been a fundamental element of civilization ever since the origin of humanity. The execution of a criminal who has been given the death penalty by a court of law for a serious offence is known as capital punishment, commonly known as the death penalty. It is regarded

as the harshest type of punishment. It is a commonly believed notion that reformist and dissuasive philosophies of punishment combine to create the basis of Indian criminal law. Applying penalties to discourage offenders is necessary, but the offender must also be given the chance to change.

The British Indian legislative assembly did not address the death penalty until 1931. During two discussions in the Legislative Assembly prior to independence, then-Home Minister Sir John Thorne made it plain what the government's position was towards the death penalty in British India. "The Government does not believe that it is prudent to repeal the death penalty for any crime for which it is currently authorised." However, the Indian Penal Code of 1860 and the Code of Criminal Procedure of 1898 were two colonial-era legislation that the Republic of India enacted after gaining its independence. Six penalties, including the death penalty, were imposed by the IPC. It is awarded in the rarest cases as held in Bachan Singh v State of Punjab 1980[i]. The Nirbhaya case[ii] and Macchi Singh case[iii] act as a testimony for this.

Sentencing offenders to death in India isn't a quick and simple process. There are numerous proceedings and trials conducted before the judge reaches such a conclusion. Ideally, there should be no delays in executing a prisoner in waiting to be executed in the death row. The IPC also permits appeal in cases where the waiting period is longer than 5 years. Approximately 488 people are now in India on death row.

Looking at death penalty in the international context, The United Nations advocated in 2007 that all its member nations eliminate the death penalty for all crimes. This concept has been rejected by several nations, including India.

There are numerous arguments in support of the death penalty as recognised by the Indian constitution. A severe punishment is required to deter murder and terrorism. By assigning the worst punishment to the worst of crimes, future offences may be deterred. This has a significant impact on psychology. It ensures delivery of justice by giving peace to the victim and their family who have been undergoing several hardships. When it comes to morality, it could be suggested that to encourage a good and just society that rejects evil, "an eye for an eye" is warranted. It is vital to instil the dread of death in the minds of criminals to enhance the atmosphere for the general public.

There have been judicial precedents favouring the constitutional validity of capital punishments in India. The death sentence was initially contested in the case of Jagmohan Singh v. State of Uttar Pradesh (1973) on the grounds that it infringed a person's right to life under Article 21[iv] of the Indian Constitution. It was decided that the death penalty is constitutionally acceptable and does not contravene any of the Constitution's articles.

In Deena Dayal v. Union of India (1983), the validity of the death sentence was once more contested on the grounds that hanging by a rope breaches Article 21 since it is barbaric, inhumane, and cruel. According to the Supreme Court, hanging is a legal and constitutional mode of execution within the limitations of Article 21. The Supreme Court affirmed the death penalty for four prisoners in the 2017 case of Mukesh and Anr. v. State (NCT of Delhi), calling it "the rarest of rare" and adding that the crime committed was appalling to humanity.

There have been cases in the past where death penalty has been justifiable hence proving that the courts are using a reasonable approach while handling this provision. The infamous Nirbhaya case where four 2012 Delhi gang members who committed rape and murder were put to death in the Tihar Jail in Delhi in March 2020, marked the most recent executions in India. Since 2000, there have only been 8 executions. Dhananjoy Chatterjee v. State of West Bengal (2004), Dhananjoy Chatterjee killed student Hetal Parekh, 18, and was found guilty of both rape and murder. He was taken into custody by Kolkata police on May 12, 1990, on suspicion of rape, murder, and watch theft and was tried in Alipore Sessions Court, found guilty of all charges, and handed a death sentence in 1991.

Kasab and nine other terrorists carried out a variety of well-planned bombing and shooting operations throughout the city during the notorious 26/11 Mumbai attack. Kasab was given the death penalty by a special court in May 2010. He should be hanged by the neck until he is dead, ordered trial judge ML Tahaliyani on May 7, adding that he had forfeited his right to "humanitarian treatment." Kasab filed a Supreme Court appeal about the death penalty in July 2011. In his statement before the court, Kasab asserted that the prosecution had not proven his guilt beyond a reasonable doubt. His appeal was denied by the Supreme Court, which confirmed the Trial Court's decision to carry out his execution on August 29, 2012.

In the current situation, where India has experienced an upsurge in rape and murder cases, where harsh actions should be taken against the perpetrators, abolishing the death sentence would not make sense. The death penalty is perceived as a more terrifying punishment than life imprisonment, thus if it were employed more frequently when the accused is fully found guilty, people would be less motivated to commit crimes.

In conclusion, there is a consequence for the perpetrator of every crime. The death sentence, which is not frequently carried out in India, is one of the adjustments. One of the rarest of the rare circumstances came into play while conducting research on death penalty convictions and capital punishment. The death penalty has long been a sensitive topic, not only on a global scale but also at the national level in India. Because execution is swift and painless, the death penalty preserves resources that might otherwise be wasted or used elsewhere if wrongdoers were just locked up or detained in prison.

Author's Bio

Kavya Srinivasan is a first year LLB (common law) student at The University of Glasgow who looks forward to gaining insights in various fields of law. Presently she is the first year rep of the Glasgow University Commercial Awareness Society and the Glasgow University Women in Law Society. She is also passionate about volunteering.

CHAPTER FOUR

THE HISTORICAL ANALYSIS OF THE COLLEGIUM SYSTEM

Author: Sankalp Shandilya, II year of B.A.,LL.B. from National Law University and judicial academy, Assam

The Law minister of India Kiran Rijuju in one of his speeches said that the "Collegium system is opaque and the government can't be silent forever" He also said "Collegium system is alien to the constitution" not only the law minister but many other politicians including citizens are showing concern on collegium system.This article tries to do a historical analysis of the collegium system. This article covers the evolution of the collegium system and the debates going around it.

<u>CONSTITUTION ON APPOINTMENT OF JUDGES</u>

Article 124(2) of the constitution of India reads (2) "Every Judge of the Supreme Court shall be appointed by the President by warrant under his hand and seal after consultation with such of the Judges of the Supreme Court and of the High Courts in the States as the President may deem necessary for the purpose and shall hold office until he attains the age of sixty-five years."

Also, article 217 of the constitution of India reads "Every Judge of a High Court shall be appointed by the President by warrant under his hand and seal after consultation with the Chief Justice of India, the Governor of the State, and, in the case of appointment of a Judge other than the Chief Justice, the Chief Justice of the High Court, and shall hold office, in the case of an additional or acting Judge, as provided in article 224, and in any other case, until he attains the age of sixty-two years."

CASE LAWS ON APPOINTMENT OF JUDGES

In S.P. Gupta v. Union of India (UOI) and Ors, 1981 Supp (1) SCC 87 popularly known as the first judge's case in this case supreme court clubbed 8 writ petitions regarding the appointment of the judge under article 139 of the constitution the question was who has power executive or judiciary to appoint judges of Supreme and High Courts and the judge gave excessive powers to the executive for appointment of judges but later this judgement was overturned In second Judges case there was friction on the issue what is the meaning of "consultation" and if the ultimate power of appointment of judges is in the hand of President then after consultancy with the council of minister president may appoint a person who is favoured by the council of ministers or loyal towards council of ministers and this will be a threat to the independence of the judiciary as well as separation of powers.

In The Supreme Court Advocates-on-Record Association (SCARA) Vs Union of India, 1993 also known as a second judges' case Supreme court overruled the judgement of the S.P Gupta case and formed a collegium system. This collegium system constitutes CJI plus two senior-most judges of the supreme court. In this judgement, it was that the word consultation doesn't limit the power of CJI in the appointment of judges. Now after this judgement executive doesn't have any say in the appointment of judges of the Supreme court and High court.

The third judges' case is not any case but an opinion given by the Supreme court on a question asked by then President K.R Narayanan after this case Supreme court expanded the number of judges from 3 to 5 in the collegium from then the collegium consist of 4 seniormost judges of Supreme court including CJI.

NJAC and the verdict of the Supreme Court

In the winter session of parliament in 2022 Vice President of India said the judgement on NJAC by SupremeCourt was a "glaring instance of severe compromise of parliamentary sovereignty and disregard of the mandate of the people". In 2016 through the 99th amendment of the constitution government introduced a National Judicial Appointment Commission for the appointment of judges of the Supreme Court and High Court but the Supreme Court in Landmark judgement of Supreme Court Advocates-on-record Association & Anr. vs. Union of India (2016) 5 SCC 1 struck down this amendment.

In this judgement, Supreme Court observed that NJAC is a threat to the Independence of the judiciary and also against the Basic Structure doctrine.

Chelameswar J. gave a dissenting opinion and claimed thatalthough the independence of the judiciary is the basic structure of theConstitution. With regards to the non-reviewable status of theSecond Judges case and Third Judges case, he states "It appears tohave been a joint venture in the subversion of the law laid down bythe 2nd Judges case and 3rd Judges case by both the executive and thejudiciary which neither party is willing to acknowledge."

The Way Forward

There is a heated debate going on between the executive and judiciary on the appointment of judges and the collegium system. A big proportion of citizens of this country also believe that the collegium system is not adequate as there is no transparency on the appointment of judges in the Supreme court and High Court. In a democracy, everything should be transparent. There are set guidelines and procedures for appointment on any post but the collegium never reveals on which basis it accepted or rejected the appointment of a particular Judge in the Supreme Court or High Court. There should be transparency regarding this. There are also allegations that due to the collegium system appointment in Higher Judiciary became dynastic as there were and are multiple Judges from the same family. Debate and Discussion area very important fabric of a healthy democracy and Chief Justice of India D.Y Chandrachud also said that "Take criticism of Collegium in a positive light, must improve." In some foreign nation take for example USA Judges are appointed by President and later confirmed by the Senate. It will be better if by mutual discussion Supreme Court and Government agrees to a common solution to this problem but it is a very tough task as No one wants to limit their power so why Judiciary will accept a proposal or a bill that will limit its power. There is also another side of this debate as in the Majority of cases Union of India is a party. If in the appointment of judiciary absolute power will be given to the government then there are chances that they will appoint those people as Judges who work in favour of the government or who will give judgement according to the wishes of the government. There is a need for a system that ensures the Independence of the Judiciary, Separation of Power and appointment of competent judges without harming the Basic structure of the constitution.

Author's Bio

Myself Sankalp Shandilya. I am a second-year student at National Law University and judicial academy Assam and I have an interest in constitutional law and the polity of India.

CHAPTER FIVE

CUSTODIAL TORTURE: AN INFRINGEMENT OF HUMAN RIGHTS

Author: Shivani Sangwan, V year of B.A.,LL.B. from Vivekananda Institute of Professional Studies, IP University

Abstract

Human rights can generally be defined as those rights which are inherent in our nature, without which we cannot live as human beings. In order to safeguard these rights and maintain law and order in society, police play a pivotal role, vested with the primary duty to maintain law and order and enforce regulations for the prevention and detection of crimes. But to discharge these legitimate duties, wide powers of arrest and investigation are vested in the police by law, but these powers are often abused by the police to torture the suspects either to solve a crime or for sadistic pleasures, which stand paradoxically in the way of the human rights of the accused. The power of investigation affords the police the occasion to perpetrate third-degree torture on the suspects to detect crimes as a matter of routine practice. These practices of brutality by the police in police custody against the detainees or the suspects have largely tarnished the image of the police, as custodial violence has become an intrinsic part of the police administration. The total range of such mistreatments is fairly vast and can spread from minor incidents of mental and physical violence to even deaths or irreparable damage to the victims. So, most democracies must have some sort of mechanism to free society from the clutches of this cruel evil both at the organisational level and also by several arrangements participated by many social service or public-spirited institutions. In the international scenario, a significant effort has been made to combat the practice of torture in all its forms, especially by law enforcement officers. Even at the national level, starting from the Indian Constitution along with other legislations, accompanied by judicial intervention in a number of significant decisions and active involvement of the National Human Rights Commission, have made worthwhile efforts to combat brutal practices of torture by the police and other law enforcement officials. But the statistics revealed that custodial violence, torture, rape and death still continue to exist as a crowning reality, flushing down all the efforts in total failure. So, in this paper, an attempt has been made to focus on the loopholes present in the existing system which perpetuates this evil of custodial torture, in spite of repeated efforts at all levels and concludes by giving a set of suggestive remedies to strike at the very root of this evil.

Introduction

Torture is considered one of the most powerful tools to extract information or extort information which sometimes also leads to the death of the person being tortured. Such deaths are quite common in India. One of the very recent incidents of custodial torture was the deaths of a father-son duo, P Jeyaraj, 62 and J Bennix, 32, from alleged police brutality during judicial custody in Tamil Nadu stirred outrage in the country. This was not a standalone case of police brutality during custody; the number of reported custodial deaths is increasing in the country at an alarming rate, as per a report published by the National Campaign Against Torture[1] around

1,723 people died in custody in India.

Torture is defined as the willful, repetitive, or cruel infliction of physical or mental pain on one or more people to force the other person to yield information or make a confession. It denotes overwhelming physical, mental, or psychological suffering that aims at thrusting one to do or say against one's own will. The Torture Commission of India attempted to define torture as "torture was fair by which guilt is punished, or confession extorted." "Torture is not merely physical; there may be mental Torture and psychological Torture calculated to create fright and submission to the demands or commands. When the threats proceed from a person in Authority and that too by a police officer, the mental torture caused by it is even more grave."[2]

Under customary international law, the prohibition of torture is jus cogens—a peremptory norm that is non-derogable under any circumstances. In 1999, the Israeli Supreme Court issued a pivotal decision declaring a number of interrogation techniques to be illegal.[3] Hon'ble Judge Shri. V.R. Krishna Iyer is of the opinion that custodial torture, in comparison to terrorism, is worse because the Authority is behind it.[4]

International Laws to Combat Custodial Torture

There is an international consensus that the abuses like custodial torture or violence violate the inherent dignity of the human being and are not justified under any circumstances. The prohibition of torture and ill-treatment, particularly in custody, is found in all major international and regional human rights treaties. At the international level, a number of significant efforts have been made which can act as important tools to fight against custodial torture.

Universal Declaration of Human Rights (UDHR)[5]

On the international platform, the first initiative that has been taken against torture is the Universal Declaration of Human Rights (UDHR), adopted on 10th December 1948, in which Article 5 laid down that no torture and other cruel, inhumane, or humiliating treatment or punishment should never be permitted. The Four Geneva Conventions adopted by the International Diplomatic Conference in 1949, although they deal principally with international armed conflicts, common Article 3 expressly prohibits torture. Additional Protocol II is relevant in the context of internal armed conflicts such as civil wars, insurgencies and low-intensity operations against armed groups. In all circumstances, torture and ill-treatment of all persons in any form of custody are strictly prohibited under Articles 4 and

5.

International Covenant on Civil and Political Rights (ICCPR)[6]

ICCPR, adopted on 16th December 1966, expressly prohibits torture, cruel, inhuman or degrading treatment or punishment under Article 7 and Article 10(1). Being convinced that further steps were needed to achieve the abolition of torture and ill-treatment worldwide, the UN General Assembly adopted a Declaration on the Protection of All Persons from being subjected to torture and other cruel, inhuman or degrading treatment or punishment on 9th December 1975, where Articles 2 and 5 strictly condemn torture. The UN Convention Against Torture and other Cruel, Inhuman or Degrading Treatment or Punishment was adopted by the UN General Assembly on 10th December 1984. It sets out the internationally accepted definition of torture and ill-treatment under Article 1 and establishes the responsibility of States for preventing these abuses under Artticles 2, 4, 10, 11, 12, 13 and 14 and provides for the creation of a Committee against Torture for the proper implementation of this Convention.

Code of Conduct for Law Enforcement Officials[7]

It was adopted by General Assembly on 17th December 1979, which made a significant effort on the international platform to prevent custodial torture and violence. According to Articles 2, 3, 5, 6, 7 and 8, law enforcement authorities are required to respect and defend human dignity as well as uphold everyone's human rights while carrying out their duties. Prohibition of Torture has been firmly established in European Human Rights Law since 1950, where the Council of Europe adopted the European Convention on human rights, whereby Article 3 expressly provides that no one shall be subjected to torture or inhuman or degrading treatment or punishment.

<u>The European Convention for the Prevention of Torture and Inhuman or Degrading Treatment or Punishment[8]</u>

The European Convention on Human Rights has been complemented by the European Convention for the Prevention of Torture and Inhuman or Degrading Treatment or Punishment adopted on 1st February 1989, which establishes the European Committee for the Prevention of Torture and Inhuman or Degrading treatment or punishment. This Committee is entitled to make visits; examine the treatment of persons deprived of liberty with a view to strengthening the protection of such persons from torture, inhuman or degrading treatment or punishment. The OSCE Budapest

Summit (1994) specifically recognised its importance, suggesting an endorsement of both its mechanism and preventive safeguards advocated by its Committee. The first protocol to this Convention, on entering into force, has also invited non-member States of the Council of Europe to join the Convention system. The Committee for the Prevention of Torture is composed of many independent and impartial members who can also be assisted by ad hoc experts. It can conduct periodic and ad hoc visits in places where custodial torture can be committed. The members of the Committee can communicate freely and without witnesses with the victims. It can also impose an obligation upon the State to cooperate in conducting its procedure of detecting cases of torture, especially in custody. Some of the other significant international efforts for the treatment of prisoners, which can be used as effective tools for the treatment of prisoners and in protecting the victims of custodial violence, are -

- UN Standard Minimum Rules for the Treatment of Prisoners, 1977.[9]
- UN Principles of Medical Ethics Relevant to the Role of Health Personnel, particularly Physicians, in the Protection of Prisoners and Detainees against Torture and other Cruel, Inhuman or Degrading Treatment or Punishment, 18th December 1982.[10]
- UN Body of Principles for the Protection of All Persons under any Form of Detention or Imprisonment, 9th December 1988.[11]
- UN Basic Principles on the Role of Lawyers, 7th September 1990.[12]
- United Nations Rules for the Protection of Juveniles Deprived of their Liberty, 14th December 1990.[13]
- UN Principles on the Effective Prevention and Investigation of Extra-legal, Arbitrary and Summary Executions, 24th May 1989.[14]
- UN basic principles on the use of force and firearms by Law Enforcement Officials, 7th September 1990.[15]
- Declaration on the protection of all Persons from Enforced Disappearance, 18th December 1992.[16]

Simply banning torture or ill-treatment in custody will not be sufficient to prevent them. Major human rights treaties establish specific Treaty-Monitoring Bodies responsible for ensuring compliance with the treaty provisions, which can also be used as effective tools for preventing custodial torture and violence.

Human Rights Committee

The International Covenant on Civil and Political Rights has established a monitoring body called the Human Rights Committee comprising of 18 independent experts, which can be significantly used as a tool to combat custodial torture. It examines reports, which the States are obliged to submit periodically and issues concluding observations that draw attention to points of concern like custodial violence and makes specific recommendations to the States. The Committee can also consider communications from the victims themselves.

The UN Committee Against Torture[17]

This Committee Against Torture is a body of 10 experts established under Article 22 of the Torture Convention, which is also another significant instrument that can be used to prevent or to protect victims of custodial torture. It considers the reports submitted by the States and issues concluding observations on the flagrant and burning issues of human rights violations like custodial violence. It may also examine communications from individuals and other public-spirited lawyers on issues of torture.

The UN Special Rapporteur on Torture and Other Cruel, Inhuman and Degrading Treatment or Punishment

This Special Rapporteur Against Torture was first established in 1985 by the UN Commission on Human Rights with the purpose of examining international practices relating to torture and reporting upon it. On the basis of the information received, it can communicate with the Governments and report their comments on cases of torture, which are raised. It can also use the "Urgent Action Procedure" requesting Governments to ensure that the victims inside police custody are treated humanely. They can also visit the police or judicial custody if necessary. This rapporteur also reports publicly to the UN Commission on Human Rights and UN General Assembly, thereby making the States more answerable or responsible for custodial torture.

In accordance with Principle 6 of the UN Basic Principles on the Independence of the Judiciary, the Judiciary has the right and obligation to ensure that court processes are conducted fairly and that the rights of the parties are respected. Article 15 of the United Nations Guidelines on the Role of Prosecutors expressly imposed an ethical duty upon the prosecutor to investigate and prosecute the crime of torture committed by public officials. All these efforts can be used as significant steps to combat custodial torture and provide protection to the victims. The Istanbul Protocol, 1999 is also a proposed standard international procedural guideline in regard to an examination of charges of torture or cruel, inhumane, or humiliating treatment or punishment. It was submitted to the United Nations in 1999 for further processing. Very detailed and methodical steps that would help the process of investigation into all such complaints against custodial torture have been made.

Another significant effort was the VIIth International Symposium on Torture as a Challenge to Health, Legal and other Professions, which was held in New Delhi from 22nd to 25th September 1999. Due to continuous and sustained efforts on the part of medical and other experts against torture, sufficient knowledge about torture, its methods and diagnostic methods have been gathered. It also helps in the rehabilitation of victims. This symposium concluded with the adoption of the "Delhi Declaration," which is a plan of action to counter the widespread menace of torture. After looking at the actions taken on the international platform, the following section discusses how India deals with the right of the accused against custodial torture, harassment and ill-treatment.

Right to the accused against custodial torture, harassment and ill-treatment in India

Much before India signed and ratified the international instruments and became a party to various UN Declarations prohibiting acts of torture, the concept of prohibition and opposition of torture, especially when committed by law enforcement officers, had been in India as early as 1860 when the Indian Penal Code[18] was enacted. Sections 330 and 331 of this Code expressly prohibit acts of torture, cruel, inhuman or degrading treatment by the police or other law enforcement officers as an offence punishable with the imposition of penalties. Besides this, under the Code of Criminal Procedure,[19] Section 163 and Police Act[20], along with Section 24 of the Indian Evidence Act,[21] have also, by law, prescribed various tasks to be fulfilled by the law enforcement agencies, which can be used as tools to prevent custodial violence. Although under Section 161 of the Code of Criminal Procedure, a police officer is entitled to examine witnesses while making an investigation, the police officer, under any circumstances, is not authorised to torture the witness before him, including the accused. Even the Indian Evidence Act of 1872 also prohibits custodial abuse or torture under Sections 24, 25 and 26.

The effect of the third degree or the subjugation and harassment of a person under custody, causing physical or mental harm, to such person, i.e., the accused or suspect, directly affects his fundamental right of freedom and is also a gross violation of Article 21 of the Indian Constitution.[22] By virtue of active judicial interpretation and activism, the Supreme Court, through a number of important judgments and landmark decisions, included under the aegis of Article 21, i.e., protection of life and personal liberty, protection against inhuman treatment, prison torture and police atrocities. Even the responsibility for preventing brutality in the police methodology was a duty on the part of the State by virtue of the equality clause under Article 14, which obligates the States to guarantee all people equality before the law or equal protection of laws.

But in spite of all these international and national efforts to combat torture, custodial torture still continues as a crowning reality. At the international level, one of the most recent cases is the gross and systematic and rampant practice of torture carried on by the American soldiers upon the Iraqi prisoners in the Abu Garib prison in Iraq, subjecting the detainees to inhuman and humiliating and degrading treatment. None of them was allowed to have prompt access to a lawyer or their family. Even a judicial review of their detention did not take place. All these reported cases were just the tip of the iceberg, as the majority of the cases escaped unnoticed or unreported. At this juncture, it is apt to focus on the attitude of the Indian Judiciary towards custodial violence and the way they handle this evil, which has been discussed in the subsequent section.

Judicial pronouncements regarding custodial torture

The Supreme Court has taken a very positive stand against police atrocities, intimidation, harassment and the use of third-degree methods to extort confession. The Court has characterised all this as being against human dignity. The expression "life" in Article 21 means the right to live with human dignity, and this includes a guarantee against torture and assault by the State. Describing police torture as disastrous to the awareness of our human rights, the Supreme Court has held that the State is responsible for remedying the situation. If police brutality is not checked at the earliest, then the credibility of the rule of law will deteriorate in our Republic.

Rajasthan Kisan Sangathan v. the State of Rajasthan[23] and Mohanlal Sharma v. State of Uttar Pradesh[24]

The Supreme Court expressly stated that if police are found to ill-treat a detenu, he would be entitled to monetary compensation under Article 21 along with punishment.

Raghubir Singh v. the State of Haryana[25]

Supreme Court asserted that it was deeply disturbed by the diabolical recurrence of police torture resulting in a terrible scare in the minds of common citizens that their lives and liberty are under new peril when the guardians of the law gore human rights to death. These observations became necessary and indispensable to impress upon the State police echelons the urgency of stamping out the vice of "third degree" from the investigative armory of the police.

Kishore Singh v. the State of Rajasthan[26]

In this case, emphasising the importance of human life underlying the spirit of Article 21, the Supreme Court strongly condemned the use of "third-degree" methods by the police. The Court further added that if the lower rungs are to truly emulate, the State must re-educate the constabulary out of their sadistic skills and inculcate a regard for the human being. This process must begin more by example than by precept. Thirdly, if any of these escort cops are found to have behaved inappropriately, the authorities should not be compelled to cover up the crime out of a sense of police comradery or in-service comity.

Anil Yadav and others v. State of Bihar and others[27]

The Supreme Court observed in this case that the blinding of accused persons in custody would amount to the most flagrant violation of safeguards provided by Articles 19 and 21. The Court was determined to bring the perpetrators of this illegal barbarity to book so that such a step would be a deterrent against similar evil-minded personnel in the hope that such brutal atrocities would not happen again.

Khatri and others v. the State of Bihar[28]

Bhagwati, J. observed that the police behaved in a most lawless manner and defied not only the constitutional safeguards but also perpetrated a crime which can be called a crime against the very essence of humanity. In Khatri (II) v. the State of Bihar, the question of compensation to be paid to the blinded victims was raised before the Supreme Court, but it was undecided as to who, in fact, particularly blinded the under-trial detenus. But however, with respect to the question of legal aid to the victims, the Supreme Court expressly held that Article 21 embodied in itself a right to legal aid to meet the requirements of "a fair, just and reasonable procedure."

Charles Sobraj v. Supdt. Jail, Tihar[29]

The Supreme Court expressly established its Authority that it can intervene with the prison administration to prevent custodial torture when the constitutional rights or statutory prescriptions are transgressed to the injury of the prisoner.

D. K. Basu v. State of West Bengal[30]

Supreme Court held that Article 21 also included within its scope, protection against custodial death and various forms of torture, cruel, inhuman and degrading treatment, and so there is a need to draw a balanced approach between the protection of fundamental rights and human rights of criminals versus duties of police with respect to custodial violence, to meet the end of justice.

Ramesh Kaushik v. Superintendent, Central Jail, New Delhi[31] and Kathi Kalu Oghad v. the State of Bombay[32]

Supreme Court held that prison torture is not beyond its constitutional jurisdiction by exercising which it can ensure some minimum social hygiene in prison. When the police and prison Torture escalated, the Court upheld that it owes a duty to society not to ignore such a dangerous reality.

Sheela Barse v. State of Maharashtra[33]

The Supreme Court asserted that prison restrictions amounting to torture, pressure or infliction and going beyond what the Court order authorised were unconstitutional. An under-trial or convicted prisoner could not be subjected to physical or mental restraint, which is not warranted by the punishment awarded by the Court or which was in excess of the requirement of the prisoner's discipline or which amounted to human degradation.

Paramvir Singh Saini v. Baljit Singh[34]

The Supreme Court has ruled that CCTV cameras must be installed in police stations and any other offices that conduct interrogations or have the authority to make arrests across the nation. The State and UT Governments were ordered by the Court to make sure that CCTV cameras are installed in each and every Police Station that is currently operational in its respective State and/or UT.

National Human Rights Commission to Curb Custodial Torture

The National Human Rights Commission (NHRC) regularly issued recommendations to combat this evil at its source in light of the rise in instances of custodial violence, custodial rape, and torture. In the Annual Report of 1997- 1998, while addressing the issue of custodial Torture, NHRC recommended:

1) Early action needs to be taken to implement the suggestion of the Indian Law Commission in its 113th report to the effect that Section 114(B) should be inserted in the Indian Evidence Act of 1872 to introduce a

rebuttable presumption that the injuries sustained by a person in the police custody may be presumed to have been caused by a police officer. Such a provision would restrain the police from engaging in torture.

2) On the basis of recommendations of the Indian Law Commission, Section 197 of the Criminal Procedure needs to be amended to eliminate the need for government sanctions for the prosecution of a police officer when a prima facie case of the commission of the custodial offence has been proven in an investigation performed by a Sessions Judge.

3) As suggested by the National Police Commission, there should be a mandatory enquiry by a Sessions Judge in each case of custodial rape, death or grievous hurt.

According to the First Annual Report of NHRC, inasmuch as 26 cases of custodial deaths or custodial rape, NHRC initiated action on its own, based on newspaper reports. On the basis of these suo motu cases, NHRC issued instructions to all State Governments and Union Territory administration on 14th December 1993 that District Magistrates or Superintendents of Police must submit reports within 24 hours of such incident, and such directions were taken care of seriously by the district authorities. NHRC also recommended payment of compensation to the next of kin of the persons killed or injured. In 1995, NHRC also visited many prisons and detention centres and made recommendations for improvement of jail conditions and felt that there was a need to replace the century-old Indian Prisons Act of 1894 and to prepare a new All-India Jail Manual, which would ensure more effective implementation of the rule of law. In the Fourth Annual Report of 1996-97, NHRC focused on civil liberties in sensitive border areas, such as custodial deaths, rape and torture. The attention of the State Human Rights Commission and Human Rights Courts is appropriate on the issue.

NHRC drafted a bill to replace the Prisons Act, recommending a wide range of measures to rationalise the prison system. NHRC issues notice to the Defence and Home Ministers on the alleged misuse of the controversial Armed Forces (Special Powers) Act, which has been vehemently criticised by various organisations.

In order to tackle the rising incidences of custodial torture, NHRC directed the Central and State Governments to take immediate steps. In its 23-page judgment, the 3-member Commission headed by J. M. N. Venkatachalam made a series of interim recommendations to be implemented. Based on such recommendations, the Government of India signed the UN Convention Against Torture and Other Cruel and Degrading Treatment or Punishment 1984. NHRC has now recommended ratification of the Convention and awaits early action in this regard, which can be used as an active instrument to prevent custodial violence and protect its victims.

Using its power under Section 12(c) of the Protection of Human Rights Act, 1993, NHRC has conducted several surprise visits, under the intimation to the State Government, to any jail or institutions under the control of the State Government, analysing the living circumstances of the detainees and make recommendations regarding them in places where people are held or accommodated for the purpose of therapy, reformation, or protection. Such visits can also help to prevent custodial violence. NHRC has also called for systematic reforms of the police. Convinced by the fact that the enforcers of law had themselves to be prevented from violating human rights, NHRC has specifically stressed the need for essential changes in the character and methods of functioning of the police and made specific proposals to this end. But in spite of these significant efforts undertaken by NHRC and the States to stop the evil of custodial violence, it continues to exist, grossly violating human rights, which shows a clear lack of political commitment to strike this evil. So, the subsequent section gives a brief picture of the ground reality, criticising the existing system and focusing on the loopholes.

Suggestions and Conclusion

The problems of custodial perversions are very complex, and merit be approached comprehensively, and a plan of action is to be sustained by continuous monitoring and relentless up-gradation of the remedial efforts. Some of the preventive steps can be:

1) The State, as well as the police administration, must make it explicit and clear that any custodial perversion will not be brook. Such a proclamation must be emphatic and assertive, and such measures must be backed up by organisational field practices that follow a desirable and professed precept.

2) Greater and closer supervision by senior police officers must be ensured. If this is not done, the very credibility of the organisation will be in peril.

3) Following the recommendations of the Third National Police Commission, there is a need for integrating the people's participation in the task of crime-fighting and efforts in this regard will be beneficial to solve the problem of custodial compulsions.

4) The workload on the police, especially on the investigator and staff in general, deserves urgent attention. Coupled with other constraints and impediments, the unfair work expectations prompt shortcuts, which lead to custodial violence. So, police work allocations should be built on scientific and modern management-oriented approaches.

5) The policy of the police organisation must be clear with regard to the "personal liability" for violations of the human rights of citizens in general and the accused in particular. Public grievance redressal must hold priority and must lie in the imagination, initiative and ability of the police leaders to take the problem of public complaints seriously and build an ethos of lawful and humane policing standards.

6) As a part of the police community relationship, an attempt must be made to provide access to the police lock-ups and records can be ventured under the direct participation of the senior police officers and carefully chosen citizens Committees.

7) Science must be fully invoked to act as a dual-purpose option as a check on the use of unjustified force on the one hand and on the other hand as documentary proof of police desire to pursue the actions strictly within the bounds of the law. So, audio and video technology during police interrogation must be used.

8) A judicial enquiry must be made mandatory in all cases of custodial deaths. The final report of judicial or Magisterial enquiry must be mandatorily published in the Official Gazette by the respective State Government soon after the receipt of the report.

9) In all cases of custodial death, post-mortem must be mandatorily conducted within 24 hours of the report of the incident. If it is not possible to meet this time limit, the concerned authorities must record in writing the reasons for the delay and ensure to take steps to complete the required post-mortem at the earliest.

10) Medical examination of the arrested accused at his instance, when produced before the Magistrate under Section 54 of the Criminal Procedure Code, 1973, must be made obligatory or mandatory in all cases of custodial violence. A copy of the medical certificate must be made available to the arrested person or his representative. Post-mortem must be done by a team of reputed doctors, not less than two. In all cases of custodial deaths, post-mortem reports must be made accessible to the relatives or family of the victim.

11) Investigation methods and documentation efforts in all cases of custodial violence must be streamlined. A specific time frame of not more than 30 days must be prescribed to finalise the investigation of the case by the police with proper preservation and maintenance of records.

12) The police must bear faithful allegiance to the Indian Constitution, and the police should uphold and respect the rights of its citizens as provided by the supreme law of India.

13) The police should recognise and respect the limitations of their powers and functions. They should not usurp the functions of the Judiciary or avenge individuals and punish the guilty. When the application of force becomes inevitable for the proper functioning of the police, only minimum force, not more than required in a given circumstance, should be used.

14) The police should always be polite and well-mannered, trustworthy and unbiased, and should possess dignity and courage and cultivate the character and trust of the people keeping in mind the welfare of the people.

15) The monetary compensation awarded to the victims of custodial torture should be saddled on the erring officials. Human rights watch groups should play a laudable role in monitoring human rights violations and bringing them to public attention.

Thus, there is a new urgency to look at custodial violence, which pragmatically makes it impossible to achieve democracy or peace, perpetuating the oppression of the accused in the hands of the police and personnel of security forces. There is a need to reconceptualise the universality and non-divisibility of human rights and rights of the accused, with radical police reform and transformation of the social attitudes towards the accused and their rights, to erase the subjection of the accused to torture or to cruel, inhuman and degrading treatment or punishment, so as to strike at the very root of this evil, before it becomes too late, as "every tomorrow is the first day of the rest of our life."

CHAPTER SIX

MAN'S BRAIN IN MACHINE

Author: Sushmitha. J, V year of B.B.A.,LL.B. from Prist University- School of Law

ABSTRACT

Artificial intelligence (AI) is a wide-ranging branch of computer science concerned with building smart machines capable of performing tasks that typically requires human intelligence.

AI is an interdisciplinary science with multiple approachesaimed at automating tasksin a need of human intelligence. And a unique innovation as an artificial entity aids to solve complicated problems. Both Computer science and Physiology are combined in Artificial Intelligence.

AI progress becomesexpeditious more robots and autonomous systems will be created replacing the human labour. AI has upperhand and benefits as its with numerous applications that would lead this planet a greater place to live. AI greatly increases the efficiency of the existing economyas its one of the fastest-growing technology that makes human life effortless by providing solutions for complex problems and even helpful in bringing different opportunities for everyone, hence been a demanding technology in the market.

On the other hand It is anticipated that AIs will affect almost everything connected to human life such as ethics, privacy, economy, employment, etc. The questionthat's constantly raising in everyone's head is abouthow to ensure itssafety in working by not causing harm to human beings and other creatures. Besides how they differ from human beings in matters concerning ethical issues associated with privacy and confidentiality.

AI is everywhere and Many of us already live and encounter it everyday, without us being aware of it. An increasing number of technological developments that we use in our day to day lives are based on AI such as from Apple's Siri, Amazon's Alexa, chatbots, Netflix, streaming services

,maps, taxi service to development of self-driving cars etc.

Some gives assumption that it will save workload and humanity, and others predict it will destroys us. Either way, if it happens, the world will be changed forever.

Keywords: Artificial intelligence(AI), machine, role, technology,Strength and weakness.

INTRODUCTION

"Artificial Intelligence- The Future is Here"

Artificial Intelligence is all about developing intelligent machines that can Simulate the human brain and work & behave like human Beings. The intelligence possessed by the machines under which they can perform various functions with human help. Artificial intelligence is a process of making computers, robots or software that can think intellectually like a human brain.

Artificial Intelligence is a combination of two words Artificial and Intelligence, which refers to man-made Intelligence. Therefore, when machines are equipped With man-made intelligence to perform intelligent tasks Similar to humans, it is known as Artificial Intelligence.

Artificial intelligence (AI), also referred to as machine intelligence, is the capability of a machine to imitate intelligent human behaviour, With the help of A.I, machines will be able to learn, solve problems, plan things, think, etc. Artificial Intelligence, for example, is the simulation of human intelligence by machines. In the field of technology, Artificial Intelligence is evolving rapidly day by day and it is believed that in the near future, artificial intelligence is drastically changing the human life.

Artificial intelligence is the theory and development of computer systems able to perform tasks that normally require human intelligence, such as visual perception, speech recognition, decision-making, and translation between languages.

HISTORICAL BACKGROUND

The researchers in the field of Al are much older. It is said that the concept of intelligent machines was found in Greek Mythology. In the year 1943, Warren McCulloch and Walter pitsProposed a model of Artificial neurons. In the year 1950, Alan Turing published a "Computer Machinery and Intelligence" paper in which he introduced a test, known as a Turing Test. This test isUsed to determine intelligence in machines byChecking if the machine is capable of thinking or not.

1956- for the first time, the term Artificial Intelligence was coined by the American Computer scientist John McCarthy at the Dartmouth Conference. John McCarthy is also known as the Father of AI. Artificial intelligence is enhancing the ability of machines to make it perform in the same way as human beings.they make the work easier, further helping to resolve a problem in a human way.

1972- the first full-scale intelligentHumanoid robot, WABOT1, was created in Japan. . In the year 1980, AI came with the evolution of Expert Systems. These systems are computer programs, which are designed to solve complex problems.

1997 – Supercomputer 'Deep Blue' was designed, and it defeated the world champion chess player in a match. It was a massive milestone by IBM to create this large computer.

2000: Professor Cynthia Breazeal developed the first robot that could simulate human emotions with its face,which included eyes, eyebrows, ears, and a mouth. It was called Kismet.

2002 – The first commercially successful robotic vacuum cleaner was created and The first Roomba was released.

2003: Nasa landed two rovers onto Mars (Spirit and Opportunity) and they navigated the surface of the planet without human intervention.

2006: Companies such as Twitter, Facebook, and Netflix started utilizing AI as a part of their advertising and user experience (UX) algorithms.

2010: Microsoft launched the Xbox 360 Kinect, the first gaming hardware designed to track body movement and translate it into gaming directions.

2011: Apple released Siri, the first popular virtual assistant.

2014: Microsoft released Cortana, their version of a virtual assistant similar to Siri on iOS. Amazon created Amazon Alexa, a home assistant that developed into smart speakers that function as personal assistants.

2016: Hanson Robotics created a humanoid robot named Sophia, who became known as the first "robot citizen" and was the first robot created with a realistic human appearance and the ability to see and replicate emotions, as well as to communicate.

2017: Facebook programmed two AI chatbots to converse and learn how to negotiate, but as they went back and forth they ended up forgoing English and developing their own language, completely autonomously.

2018: Samsung introduced Bixby, a virtual assistant. Bixby's functions include Voice, where the user can speak to and ask questions, recommendations, and suggestions; Vision, where Bixby's "seeing" ability is built into the camera app and can see what the user sees (i.e. object identification, search, purchase, translation, landmark recognition); and Home, where Bixby uses app-based information to help utilize and interact with the user (e.g. weather and fitness applications.) A Chinese tech group called Alibaba's language-processing AI beat human intellect on a Stanford reading and comprehension test.

2019: Google's AlphaStar reached Grandmaster on the video game StarCraft 2, outperforming all but .2% of human players.

2020: OpenAI started beta testing GPT-3, a model that uses Deep Learning to create code, poetry, and other such language and writing tasks. While not the first of its kind, it is the first that creates content almost indistinguishable from those created by humans. Baidu releases the LinearFold AI algorithm to medical and scientific and medical teams developing a vaccine during the early stages of the SARS-CoV-2 (COVID-19) pandemic. The algorithm can predict the RNA sequence of the virus in only 27 seconds, which is 120 times faster than other methods.

2021: OpenAI developed DALL-E, which can process and understand images enough to produce accurate captions, moving AI one step closer to understanding the visual world.

2022- Operational AI, Model Ops, AI cloud, Smart robots, Natural language processing, Automotive vehicles. Intelligent applications and computer vision.

Including playing Atari, captioning images and using a robotic arm to stack blocks.

Importance of AI

Machine or software intelligence is referred to as artificial intelligence.

Perceive + Analyse + React = Intelligence.

Artificial intelligence is a subject of computer science that is rapidly gaining popularity since it has improved human existence in a variety of ways.

Artificial intelligence has substantially enhanced the performance of manufacturing and service systems during the previous two decades.

Prior to the current wave of AI, it would have been hard to imagine using computer software to connect riders to taxis, but today Uber has become one of the largest companies in the world by doing just that. It utilizes sophisticated machine learning algorithms to predict when people are likely to need rides in certain areas, which helps proactively get drivers on the road before they're needed. As another example, Google has become one of the largest players for a range of online services by using machine learning to understand how people use their services and then improving them.

Artificial intelligence forms the basis for all computer learning and is the future of all complex decision making. Today's largest and most successful enterprises have used AI to improve their operations and gain advantage on their competitors.

It enables human capabilities by understanding, reasoning, planning, communication and perception and to be undertaken by software increasingly effectively, efficiently and at low cost.AI can be applied to every sector to enable new possibilities and efficiencies.

"Artificial intelligence is about replacing human decision making with more sophisticated technologies." – Falguni Desai.

<u>CATEGORIES OF AI</u>

REACTIVE- Has no memory, only responds to different stimuli. An example of Reactive AI is the famous IBM Chess program that beat the world champion, Garry Kasparov

LIMITED MEMORY- Uses memory to learn and improve its responses. For example, self-driving cars use sensors to identify civilians crossing the road, steep roads, traffic signals and so on to make better driving decisions. This helps to prevent any future accidents.

THEORY OF MIND- Understands the needs of other intelligent entities. This has not yet been fully developed but rigorous research is happening in this area.

SELF-AWARE-Has human-like intelligence and self-awareness.

Branches Of Artifical Intelligence

Artificial Intelligence can be used to solve real-world problems by implementing the following processes/ techniques:

Machine Learning - the science of getting machines to interpret, process and analyze data in order to solve real-world problems.There are three types of machine learning algorithms:

Supervised learning- Data sets are labeled so that patterns can be detected and used to label new data sets.

Unsupervised learning- Data sets aren't labeled and are sorted according to similarities or differences.

Reinforcement learning- Data sets aren't labeled but, after performing an action or several actions, the AI system is given feedback.

2. Natural Language Processing - the science of drawing insights from natural human language in order to communicate with machines and grow businesses. Ex: Twitter uses NLP to filter out terroristic language in their tweets, Amazon uses NLP to understand customer reviews and improve user experience.

3. DeepLearning - Deep Learning is an advanced field of Machine Learning that can be used to solve more advanced problems. Ex: face verification algorithm on Facebook, self-driving cars, virtual assistants like Siri, Alexa etc.

4. Expert Systems - an AI-based computer system that learns and reciprocates the decision-making ability of a human expert. Ex: information management, medical facilities, loan analysis, virus detection

5. Fuzzy Logic- Fuzzy logic is a computing approach based on the principles of "degrees of truth" instead of the usual modern computer logic i.e. boolean in nature. Ex- automatic gearboxes, vehicle environment control and in medical field to solve complex problems,

6. Robotics- focuses on different branches and application of robots. AI Robots are artificial agents acting in a real-world environment to produce results by taking accountable actions. Ex: Sophia the humanoid

TYPES OF AI

Artificial Narrow Intelligence (ANI)- Also known as Weak AI, ANI is the stage of Artificial Intelligence involving machines which can perform only a narrowly defined set of specific tasks. At this stage, the machine does not possess any thinking ability, it just performs a pre-defined set of functions. Examples- Siri, Alexa, Self-driving cars, Alpha-Go, Sophia the humanoid and so on. Almost all the AI-based systems built till this date fall under the category of Weak AI.

Artificial General Intelligence (AGI)-Also known as Strong AI, AGI is the stage in the evolution of Artificial Intelligence wherein machines will possess the ability to think and make decisionslikehuman being. Strong AI is considered as a threat to human existence by many scientists.

Artificial Super Intelligence (ASI)- It is the stage of Artificial Intelligence when the capability of computers will surpass human beings. ASI is a hypothetical situation presently depicted in movies, sci-fi books, where machines have taken control over the world.

STRENGTHS

" Our intelligence is what makes us human, and AI is an extension of that quality." – Yann LeCun

AI has the potential to cross the boundaries of capital and labour and open up new sources of value and growth.

The advantages of Artificial intelligence applications are enormous and can revolutionize any professional sector.

Reduction in Human Error like in Weather Forecasting using AI they have reduced the majority of human error.

Available 24x7 like Educational Institutes and Helpline centre's are getting many queries and issues which can be handled effectively using AI.

Helping in Repetitive Jobs example in banks, we often see many verifications of documents to get a loan which is a repetitive task for the owner Using AI Cognitive Automation the owner can speed up the process for verifying the documents by which both the customers and the owner will be benefited.

Medical applications

Takes risks instead of Humans AI Robot which can do the risky things for us like going to mars, defuse a bomb, explore the deepest parts of oceans, mining for coal and oil, it can be used effectively in any kind of natural or man-made disasters.

Faster Decisions

Daily applications such as Apple's Siri, Window's Cortana, OKGoogle are frequently used in our daily routine whether it is for searching a location, taking a selfie, making a phone call, replying to a mail and many more.

Digital Assistance in case of Using AI the organizations can set up a Voice bot or Chatbot which can help customers with all their queries.

The advantages of Artificial Intelligence also include planning, learning, reasoning and problem-solving abilities. Human intelligence stimulated Artificial Intelligence as an effective way to substitute automation of machines. AI is the fastest growing field in terms of technology and Innovation. As every bright side has a darker version in Below are the Cons of AI.

WEAKNESSES

"The future is ours to shape. I feel we are in a race that we need to win. A race between the growing power of the technology and the growing wisdom we need to manage it." -Max Tegmark

Artificial Intelligence is becoming the synonym for future. In a world dominated by machines, machine minds and machine hearts, everything is based on technology. To gain control over technology is the task of Artificial Intelligence. Created with extraordinary human intelligence, Artificial

Intelligence or Al is a substitute for tasks that could be done with combined human efforts and machine involvement. No wonder that this phenomena will rule the future, as every little aspect in the field of everyday technology is affected by Al in one way or another.

Unemployment

Lacking Out of Box Thinking

High cost

No matter how smart a machine becomes, it can never replicate a human. Machines are rational but, very inhuman as they don't possess emotions and moral values.

Creativity is not the key for AI as Machines can't be creative. They can only do what they are being taught or commanded.They can never match the power of human brain.

Lacking Improvement

Ethics and morality are important human features that can be difficult to incorporate into an AI.

ROLE OF AI IN EACH FIELD

AI Applications are found in various domains. There are a number of industries which are on the verge of transformation by AI .

Agriculture

Artificial Intelligence has a major role to play in driving a food revolution and meeting the increased demand for food. Applied Artificial Intelligence addresses challenges such as lack of assured irrigation, inadequate demand prediction, excess use of pesticides, fertilizers, and fungicides. Some uses include better crop production through detecting pest attacks, forecasting crop prices, and real-time advice.

Manufacturing

It can enable flexible and adaptable technical systems to facilitate various processes and machinery to respond to unfamiliar or unpredictable situations by making "smart decisions" through flexible and adaptable technical systems. Areas of influence include engineering, supply chain management, production, maintenance, quality assurance, and plant logistics and warehousing.

Automobile- At this stage where automobiles changing from an engine with a chassis around it to a software-controlled intelligent machine, the role of AI cannot be underestimated. The goal of self-driving cars, during which Autopilot by Tesla has been the frontrunner, takes up data from all the Tesla's running on the road and uses it in machine learning algorithms.

Gaming-In the gaming industry also , computer game Systems powered by AI is ushering us into a replacement era of immersive experience in gaming.AI has also been playing a huge role in creating video games and making it more tailored to players' preferences.

Matthew Guzdial from the University of Alberta and his team are working towards leveraging AI's power to assist video gamers create the precise game that they need to play.

Healthcare

Artificial Intelligence plays an important role in the field of healthcare by addressing issues of high barriers, particularly in rural areas that lack poor communication and a professional healthcare system. Some of the emerging applications include AI-driven diagnostics, personalized treatment, early detection of potential epidemics, and imaging diagnostics.

Surveillance- AI has made it possible to develop face recognition Tools which may be used for surveillance and security purposes.Manual monitoring of a CCTV camera requires constant human intervention so they're prone to errors and fatigue. AI-based surveillance is automated and works 24/7, providing real-time insights.

According to a report by the Carnegie Endowment for International Peace, a minimum of 75 out of the 176 countries are using AI tools for surveillance purposes.

Retail

Being one of the early adopters of Artificial Intelligence solutions, it provides applications such as developing user experience by personalized suggestions, image-based product search, and preference-based browsing.

Education and Skilling- Artificial Intelligence provides the need for student intervention to provide solutions to quality and accessibility issues in the Indian education sector and enhance the learning experience through personalized learning, automate and expedite administrative tasks, and reduce dropouts.

Banking and Finance- One of the early adopter of Artificial Intelligence is the Banking and Finance Industry. Features like AI bots, digital payment advisers and biometric fraud detection mechanisms cause higher quality of services to a wider customer base.

The adoption of AI in banking is constant to rework companies within the industry, provide greater levels useful and more personalized experiences to their customers, reduce risks as well as increase opportunities involving financial engines of our modern economy.

Smart Cities

The incorporation of applied Artificial Intelligence in developing cities could also help in meeting the demands of a rapidly growing population and providing them with enhanced quality of life. Traffics control for reducing congestion enhanced security by providing improved crowd management are some of the potential uses of Artificial Intelligence systems.

Space Exploration: AI systems are being developed to scale back the danger of human life that venture into the vast realms of the undiscovered and unraveled universe which is a very risky task that the astronauts need to take up. Has helped us discover numerous exoplanets, stars, galaxies, and more recently, two new planets in our very own system.

Entertainment- The show business , with the arrival of online streaming services like Netflix and Amazon Prime, relies heavily on the info collected by the users.With new contents being created every minute , it is very difficult to classify them and making them easier to search.

AI tools analyze the contents of videos frame by frame and identify objects to feature appropriate tags. AI is additionally helping media companies to form strategic decisions.

E-Commerce- This is one of the Artificial Intelligence Applications that's found to be widely used. E-commerce retailers are increasingly turning towards chatbots or digital assistants to supply 24×7 support to their online buyers. Built using AI technologies, chatbots are becoming more intuitive and are enabling a far better customer experience.

AI in Judiciary

Recently, the Law Minister has said that for implementing phase two of the eCourts project, there is a need to adopt new, cutting edge technologies of Machine Learning (ML) and Artificial Intelligence (AI) to increase the efficiency of the justice delivery system.

Also, to explore the use of AI in the judicial domain, the Supreme Court of India has constituted an Artificial Intelligence Committee.The committee has identified application of AI technology in Translation of judicial documents, Legal research assistance and Process automation.

Whether Advocates are being replaced by AI?

NO AI can never replace advocate

Artificial Intelligence IS MAN WITH MACHINE And NOT MAN VS. MACHINE

AI acts only on the basis of the given data and the merits of the facts. It cannot manipulate such data. All AI can do, is to aid the lawyers, judges, magistrates or law students, to achieve a data driven result in a expeditious and inexpensive manner. It takes real humans to actually argue in the court and it is not a task that automated software can perform. AI is not replacing lawyers or rendering them out of jobs.

Positives

Artificial Intelligence and law mainly deal with the application of algorithms to make law more logical, convenient and probable.

Pendency of Cases: The recent National Judicial Data Grid (NJDG) shows that 3,89,41,148 cases are pending at the District and Taluka levels and 58,43,113 are still unresolved at the high courts. AI helps solving casesexpeditiously.

Time saving

Cost effective

Focus more on complex problems

Making decisions for complex problems

Better skill development

Efficiency in document review

Algorithms based prediction

Drafting and contract analysis

Legal research

Loopholes

Infringement of data privacy. Everything digital is subject to gross data privacy issues.

No ethical values will be followed.

The more autonomous softwares becomes, the tougher it will be for humans to handle those softwares and the results that they produce. AI cannot take over the liability.

No legal identity

Only acts on what is fed, cannot act spontaneously according to the situation and circumstances.

Competition law

Examples of AI used in judicial field

Virtual Hearing: Over the course of the Covid-19 pandemic, the use of technology for e-filing, and virtual hearings has seen a dramatic rise.

SUVAS (Supreme Court Vidhik Anuvaad Software): It is an AI system that can assist in the translation of judgments into regional languages.Which is easier to explain for a person of different languages.

SUPACE (Supreme Court Portal for Assistance in Court Efficiency): It was recently launched anfd Designed to first understand judicial processes that require automation, it then assists the Court in improving efficiency and reducing pendency being automated through AI.

UNDER INDIAN CONSTITUTION

Under Article 21 of the Constitution, the 'right to life and personal liberty' In the leading case of R Rajagopal v. State of Tamil Nadu, the right to privacy was held to be implicit under Article 21 and is relevant with addressing privacy issues arising out of AI in processing personal data. Further, in the landmark case of K.S. Puttaswamy v. Union of India, the Supreme Court emphasised the need for a comprehensive legislative framework for data protection, which shall be competent to govern emerging issues such as the use of AI in India. AI may also be unfair and discriminatory and will attract Articles 14 and 15, which deal with the right to equality and right against discrimination respectively to protect the fundamental rights of the citizens.

UNDER THE CONSUMER PROTECTION ACT, 2019

Section 83 of this Act entitles a complainant to bring an action against a manufacturer or service provider or seller of a product for any harm caused because of defective product. This establishes liability for the manufacturer or seller of an AI entity for harm caused by it.

UNDER THE PATENT ACT,1970

Patentability of AI, inventorship, ownership and liability for AI's acts/ omissions, are some of the main issues with regard to AI. Section 6 r/w Section 2(1)(y) of the Act does not specifically mandate that 'person' must be a natural person, At present, AIL has not been granted legal personhood and would not fall within the scope of the act.

UNDER THE INFORMATION TECHNOLOGY ACT, 2000

Section 43A of this Act imposes liability on a body corporate, dealing with sensitive personal data, to pay compensation when it fails to adhere to reasonable security practices. This has a significant bearing in determining the liability a body corporate when it employs AI to store and process sensitive personal data.

UNDER TORT LAW

The principles of vicarious liability and strict liability are relevant to the determination of liability for wrongful acts or omissions of AI. In the case of Harish Chandra v. Emperor, the court laid down that there is no vicarious liability in criminal law as one's wrongful acts if the AI entity may be considered as an agent.

UNDER THE PERSONAL DATA PROTECTION BILL, 2019

The processing of personal data of Indian citizens by public and private bodies located within and outside India is regulated in this bill. 'consent' for processing of such data by data fiduciaries, subject to certain exemptions. When enacted into law, this bill will affect the wide application of AI software that collects user information from various online sources to track the Consumer details relating to purchase, online content, finance etc.

CONCLUSION

AI has already impacted lives of people in various fields and will surely continue to do more in the future. It's still on the rise. Many organizations are using AI to enhance their user experience, performance, or efficiency. We cannot totally depend on a machine to replace human source. It is necessity of using within limits as probably AI is the fastest-growing development in the World of technology and innovation. Thus, we should handle and shape our future in most secure and safe way by taking over their benefits. Every new invention has some positive and negative aspects but we must use the positive aspects of the invention to create a better world.

"The Potentialbenefits ofArtificial Intelligence are huge, soare the dangers"

-Dave Waters

CHAPTER SEVEN

LEGALIZATION OF MARIJUANA: NEED AND CHALLENGES

Author: Pranshutosh kumar, II year of B.A.,LL.B.(Hons.) from University of Petroleum and Energy Studies.

Introduction

Over the years, there have been many debates and several discussions on whether there should be the legalization of Cannabis in all over the world.

It has been become a subjective issue of many states. Different countries has its own opinion on the use necessitating its legalism, all these opinion raises the question about the status of cannabis. Slicing through party lines, education, gender and race, people of different countries started raising their voice in favour of legalization of Marijuana. And some are also in opinion to remove the idea of legalization from the society. That's why this concept has become and becoming most controversial and debating topic.

Marijuana and its legal status in India

Cannabis is a herbal drug. It has the elements of cannabinoids including delta-9 tetrahydrocannabinol [THC] and cannabidiol [CBD]. The derived leaves, flowers, steam and seeds of the cannabis sativa or cannabis Indica plant are referred to as Marijuana. THC, as well as other mind- altering chemical are found in the plant. Cannabis extracts can also be created. Don't be perplexed hemp with cannabis. Hemp contains and made up of very small quantity of THC, which is less than 0.3% according to the legal standards. Hemp and cannabis are made up of cannabinoids like, CBD, cannabidgeral [CBG], cannabidivarin [CBVD] and many more. Cannabis is banned under federal law in the United Nation. It is a schedule 1 restricted drug. However, several states have allowed decriminalized recreational usage.

The status of Marijuana in India as per the legal basis is covered under the Narcotic Drug and Psychotropic Substance Act, 1955,Cannabis is found in various forms like charas, ganja,has hish bhang etc. All these forms are banned and keeping these are deemed to be unlawful. Narcotic Drug and Psychotropic Substance Act [NDPS Act], 1985. It covered cannabis along with other present narcotic and psychotropic substances.

NDPS Act 1955, define cannabis in section 2[iii], which says that cannabis (hemp) means—

A. Charas, that is, the separated resin, in whatever form, whether crude or purified, obtained from the cannabis plant and also includes concentrated preparation and resin known as hashish oil or liquid hashish;

B. Ganja, that is, the flowering or fruiting tops of the cannabis plant (excluding the seeds and leaves when not accompanied by the tops), by whatever name they may be known or designated; and

C. Any mixture, with or without any neutral material, of any of the above forms of cannabis or any drink prepared therefrom;

But bhang is not confine in this act because it is only treated or suppose as a preparation of cannabis. The National Policy on Narcotics and

Psychotropic Substances notes this reality and continues by saying that the-'production and sale of Bhang is permitted by many State Governments'.

This is discussed by various courts in many cases like, Sevaramvs State Of Rajasthan[1]. Arjun Singh vs State Of Haryana[2]. Madhukar S/O PandurangKanthalevs The State Of Maharashtra, Summons[3].

Arguments in Favor of Legalizing Marijuana

The intended Medical Welfare of Marijuana turn out be peruse by different scientific researchers and their research are resulted absolute by many studies. Study says that marijuana helps in relieve pain, nausea and muscle spam. Many people who are treated by the help of Marijuana believed that it gives faster result and also be of the opinion that it is one of the best treatment of there medical conditions.

Medical cannabis is commonly used to treat insomnia, anorexia and autism and is also linked to cancer treatment such as chemotherapy. Legalized cannabis can also be used to treat anorexia. The direct benefitsof medical cannabis are evident in the regulation of emotions and moods. Marijuana has been proved to have minimal side effect when used in strictly regulated amounts.Colorado and Washington are the two states were the first time marijuana was legalized in 2012. Marijuana legalization is additionally anticipated to spice up the country economic process.

Some happened in Colorado and Washington where the economy benefited by legalized Marijuana are often towering $300 a year. State government also covered retain large amount of taxes if they try to legalize the Marijuana. State government also lay out plenty of cash on enforcement departments liable for maintaining marijuana related laws. Numerous people are investigated and apprehend on annual basis for use and possession of marijuana and government also spent lot of money to stay them in prison. So that money can also be save and used as a welfare for the people.

Reasons against legalizing marijuana

By understanding recent political and social realities, legalization of Marijuana is not a right step for any country.There has been a shift in the cultural attitudes towards the use of marijuana for medical and recreational use. As marijuana is legalized, extreme and growing literature has been documented indicating its potential have hostile and favourable on individual and public health. The term Medical Marijuana means Marijuana is some as other drug which is determine by a doctor but the medical marijuana is ratified and released to the large public is totally dissimilar from other over- the- counter presciption drugs. There the problem which is not recognized by the general public and many doctors.

Medical use of Marijuana- Marijuana is the only medication which is smoked, at some times as nevertheless incompletely understood there are valid worries approximately for long time period results of marijuana smoked the lungs compared with the cigarette smoke. Marijuana smoke can bring about three instance the quantity of inhaled for and four instances the quantity ofinhaled carbon-monoxide. It is proven to be danger thing for lungs because it causes cancer.

High potential for diversion- There are some states has permitted patients to grow marijuana. So by looking this facts there is a high chance of drug diversion. There may be also a problem that is in the hide of good utilization patients can grow large amount of marijuana and sell them at low price in comparison to dispensaries.

Myth potential for diversion- There are many people who believe that consumption of marijuana is not addictive. Data demonstrates unequivocally that 10% of cannabis userdevelopsaddiction, the proportion is higher among teens. On average marijuana user who seek addiction treatment have used the drug regularly for ten year. There is a withdrawal syndrome that has been identified, which can impact up to 44% of frequent uses and includes symptoms like anxiety, rest lessness, insannia, depression and changes in appetite. This condition has been linked to the drugs propensity for addiction.

Marijuana also impact Schizophrenia and other psychotic disorders, cognition effect, decrease the level of respiratory system, effect on driving which has the social safety implication. The detrimental effect of marijuana on the brain in long term use of marijuana can cause memoryloss. It complicated one's sense of balance by corrupting the cerebellum. There are high chances of depression from heavy regular doses of marijuana.

<u>Conclusion</u>

The use of Marijuana in now very common in clinical practice in many states and it is critical for health cause provides to understood both the scientific rationale and the physical marijuana has been at time controversial issue, metal health provides a responsibility to provide evidence based guidance on this important issues. It can be difficult from one people to take a side in the fight over legalizing marijuana. Both points of view are supported by credible evidences and arguments. Although advocates for legalization claim that marijuana usage has health benefits, there are other medical therapies for the some ailments this making it legal for anybody to consume it isn't a compelling enough justification.

Author's Bio

Hello everyone, Myself Pranshutosh Kumar. I am from Jokwa Khurd, Kushinagar. Currently I am pursuing BA LLB {hons} from UPES Dehradun. I have interest in Researching in law field and keen to know new things.

CASE ANALYSIS OF PHONEPE V/S BHARATPE

Author: Adina Evangeline G, III year of B.A.,LL,B. from Kristu Jayanti College of Law

<u>FACTS OF THE CASE</u>

PhonePe is an online payment app that lets anyone who downloads the app use it. BharatPe is also an online payment app but is only for merchants and it also grants loans to them. Some time back, a Single Judge Bench of the Delhi High Court comprising of Mr Justice C. Hari Shankar, pronounced a notable judgment in a marketable suit filed between Phonepe(P)Ltd. v. Ezy Services on 15th April, 2021, the complainant sued the defendant for the use of the suffix 'Pe' in mark as it amounted to violation of the registered mark 'PhonePe' and passing off

In respect of payment services ordinary or in any other manner which may amount to the violation of the complainant's trade mark[1]. It is important to note that the defendants' services are available simply to merchandisers whereas the plaintiff's services are available to anyone who downloads their app. The court dismissed the petition and denied to grant injunction against the defendant. The court held that the parties cannot misspell general words and hold exclusivity over them especially at the prima facie stage unless they have acquired a secondary meaning through nonstop marketable use, which the Honourable High Court has held to be a matter of trial and substantiation when the case is to be eventually heard and decided[2]. The defendants were still directed to show the accounts of the profit earned using the 'Bharatpe' mark and to present the audit statements of six months before the court. In this case study, we will be looking at the interim order issued by the Delhi High Court in a trademark violation and passing off disagreement between online payment apps PhonePe and BharatPe, arguments by complainant and defendants, and crucial compliances of court.

ISSUE

Can PhonePe demand the permanent injunction of BharatPe from using 'Pe' in its suffix?

ARGUMENTS

ARGUMENTS BEHALF OF THE PLAINTIFF

The complainant pled before the Delhi High Court that an ordinary person on coming across the mark 'bharatpe' would associate it with the mark of 'PhonePe.'

The plaintiff had started using the mark 'PhonePe' by 2015 whereas 'BharatPe' was used only from 2018 which clearly gave enough time for the plaintiff's trademark to establish their goodwill and reputation in the market.

The plaintiff's trademark was registered prior to the defendant's and ever since then the plaintiff's app has been downloaded more than 10 crore time.

The 'pe' in the plaintiff's trademark is an important and relevant feature is what was claimed by the plaintiff.

Along with it the plaintiff also claimed that the word 'phone' was a normal dictionary word whereas the 'pe' is an invented word which distinguishes it from others and thus plays the bigger role in the trademark 'phonepe.'

Over the years the plaintiff's trademark has gained sufficient goodwill and reputation which is seen in advertisements, partnerships, articles and by their active involvement in IPL 2019 and are endorsed by various celebrities[3].

The services provided by the defendant are same as that of the plaintiff and it has also copied the distinguishing trademark suffix 'pe' of the plaintiff's trademark 'PhonePe' which amounts to infringement and passing off.

ARGUMENTS BEHALF OF THE DEFENDANT

"पे" or "Pe" as standalone marks were never used by neither the plaintiff nor the defendant in their business.

The mark 'BharatPe' was adopted and used from 2016 and later the domain name <www.bharatpe.com> was registered on 15-11-2017 in the name of its founder and in 2018 the online payment services began with a bona fide interest.

The 'BharatPe' trademark was invented by the defendants and is inherently different from the services which the plaintiff provides, also many companies use the suffix 'pay' in their names such as Google Pay, Amazon Pay, Samsung Pay etc.

The tagline "Bharat pe sab chalta hai" was used by the defendants as the idea behind this was to start a single quick response (QR) code for merchants which would work across all consumer unified payments interface (UPI)-based applications, such as Google Pay, Paytm, WhatsApp Pay, Amazon Pay etc.

The "BharatPe" app had been downloaded more than 50 lakh times till the end 2020.

In order to raise objections under Section 11 of the Trademarks Act, 1999, while examining the defendants "BharatPe" marks, did not cite any of the plaintiff's marks as an earlier trademark in the first examination report, issued by the Trademarks Registry[4].

Prior to the "PhonePe" marks of the plaintiff, involving "Pe", such as "Phone Pe Deal" "Phone Pe Store" etc, these earlier marks claimed that there were users prior to the plaintiff in registered trademarks. Therefore, the plaintiff could not claim to be the first one to use the "Pe"mark.

The suffix "Pe" was merely a misspelling of the word "Pay" and is an invented word which was admitted by the plaintiff. Phonetically, "Pe" and

"Pay" are identical. The idea behind using the suffix "Pe" was to enable the consumer to phonetically pronounce the dictionary word 'Pay'. Such misspellings, does not give any enforceable rights, where the original term is descriptive in nature. No exclusive rights can be enforced, in respect of such a misspelt word, unless the word has acquired a secondary meaning with respect to the plaintiff's business.

The suffix "Pe" was common to the trade and services provided by the plaintiff which was to enable the consumer to pay using the plaintiff's app.

LAW

(a) THE ANTI-DISSECTION RULE

Section 17(3) deals with the aftermath of the registration of parts of a mark. In the present case the complainant has not individually registered any allegedly infringed "PhonePe" mark which is why the provision assumes significance. Section 17 (1) specifically confers the right to the owner of a registered trade mark, "consisting of several matters", the exclusive rights "to the use of the trade mark taken as a whole"[5].

The "anti- dissection" rule is that the conflicting composite marks are to be compared by looking at them, rather than breaking the marks up into their component parts for comparison. The reason behind this is the that an ordinary consumer looks at the mark as a whole and not in parts. Therefore, conflicting marks must be compared in their wholeness.

The anti-dissection rule is based upon an observation of customer behaviour that the the typical shopper does not retain all the individual details of a composite mark in his or her mind, but retains only an overall, general impression created by the composite mark as a whole. The overall impression created by the mark from the ordinary shopper's observation in the marketplace is what may or may not lead to a likelihood of confusion and not the impression created from a neat and careful comparison as in legal analysis.

The court referred to a Supreme Court case the Kaviraj Pandit Durga Dutt Sharma case where the Court held that trademarks were to be compared as a whole[6].

(b) DOMINANT TEST

Here the court referred to a judgment of the Delhi High Court in South India Beverages where the 'dominant mark' test was explained by the court.

The test was to see whether any part of the plaintiff's mark was dominant or was an important feature, and if so, whether such dominant part was infringed by the defendant. The court ruled that there may be substance to the claim that 'Pe' constituted a dominant part or important feature of the marks, because it was written with a capital 'P.'

Keeping in mind the Anti-Dissection Rule if a "dominant part" of the plaintiff's mark is copied by the defendant, then the court shallintrospect ifinfringement has taken place by such imitation.

(c) NON-EXCLUSIVITY OF DESCRIPTIVE MARKS

The court held that though exclusivity cannot be claimed in parts of a registered mark, imitations of the dominant parts of such registered marks could be infringement. Misspelling descriptive words will not grant exclusivity and neither will descriptive marks.

The court held that if the plaintiff was able to prove that they had acquired second meaning then a case of infringement could have been made.

In the Marico case the court held that the descriptive mark should be given trademark only if it has been there for many years and even a descriptive word mark would be only associated with the same source[7].

CONCLUSION

The case of PhonePe vs BharatPe mentions that the plaintiff's app was used to make online payments and used by customers whereas the defendant's app was a QR based app for merchants and it had options for all UPI online payments within the app including the plaintiff's app and thus both the apps differed in services. Additionally, the suffix 'pe' is the only thing similar in both the apps and apart from it there is nothing that is deceptive, similar, or confusing. The names of the apps 'Phonepe' and 'Bharatpe' are both composite words and thus cannot be separated into 'Phone' and 'pe,' 'Bharat' and 'pe.' The plaintiff cannot claim exclusivity or infringement solely on the suffix 'pe' as it has not been registered for trademark separately[8]. 'Pe' is a misspelling of the English word 'pay' and is an invented word and thus is not eligible for exclusivity. "Phonepe" and "Bharatpe" are not even phonetically similar in order to claim infringement. For a part of the word to get exclusivity it should have been in use from a long period of time and the general public should be able to associate it with the same source but this is not the case here. From the judgement given that permanent injunction cannot be granted against the defendant for infringement by the single Judge Bench, took place after considering the case considering the anti-dissection rule, test of dominant mark and non-exclusivity of descriptive marks in the Indian Trademark law. Thus, permanent injunction will not be granted against BharatPe.This Judgement provides deep insight into the trademark laws, legal principles and serves as a precedent for the future cases to come.

Author's Bio

Adina Evangeline G is currently a 3rd year student of BA LLB, of Kristu Jayanti College of Law. Her areas of interest include Human rights, women's rights, family law, criminal law and International relations.

WAR OF WORLDS IN THE COURSE OF INDRA SAWHNEY'S CASE

Author: Ojasvi Rana, IV year of B.A.,LL.B. from Ajeenkya Dy Patil University

Title of the Case: Indra Sawhney Etc. vs Union of India and Others 1992

Citation: AIR 1993 SC 477, 1992 Supp 2 SCR 454 Court: Supreme Court of India

Bench: M Kania, M Venkatachaliah, S R Pandian, . T Ahmadi, K Singh, P Sawant, R Sahai, B J Reddy

INTRODUCTION

The topic of reservations has long been a source of controversy in India. It has had periods when educational and employment distinctions were based on social standing, class, and capitalist relations rather than on merit and fair competition. One of the essential rights given to all Indian citizens by the Indian Constitution is the right to equality. The Constitution's Article 16 addresses the issue of opportunity equality for those seeking public employment.

The Janta Party government, headed by Prime Minister Shri Morarji Desai, formed the Socially and Educationally Backward Classes (SEBC) Commission on January 1, 1979. It is now chaired by Shri B.P. Mandal. In accordance with Article 340 of the Indian Constitution, the President of India appointed this commission. In January 1953, the first SEBC commission was constituted under the leadership of Kaka Kalelkar. On March 30, 1955, it published a report citing guidelines established by the Central Government that described 2399 people as having social and educational disadvantages.

The Mandal commission delivered its findings in December 1980. In it, the committee identified 27 castes as being socially and educationally backward classes, out of a total of 3743.

On August 13, 1990, Prime Minister V.P. Singh issued an office memorandum reserving 27 seats for the Socially & Backward classes. This led to a civil unrest throughout the nation as anti-reservation sentiment spread throughout the nation.

ISSUE

Is the classification based on caste or on economic factors?

Whether or not Article 16 (4)[1] is an exception to Article 16 (1)[2]

Whether backward classes in Article 16 (4) are similar to SEBCS in Article 15 (4) or not?

Is it necessary to make "any provision" for reservation "by the state" under Article 16(4) by law passed by the state legislatures or by law passed by parliament? Is it possible that such provisions could be made by executive order?

Is the division of the backward class into backward and more backward classes valid or not?

RULE

Several times, the Supreme Court has addressed arguments regarding reservations in our Constitution.A Government Order (G.O.) issued by the State of Madras that allotted seats in engineering and medical colleges based on one's caste was challenged in the Supreme Court in State of Madras v. Smt. Champakan Dorairajan. The case was heard by a Special Bench of seven judges. The ineligibility created by the 'communal G.O.,' in which a Brahmin who was otherwise eligible was rendered ineligible due to his caste, was found to be in violation of Article 15 and 16.

The Supreme Court considered the scope of Article 16 (4) in T. Devadasan v. Union of India. The Supreme Court declared the carry forward rule, which was enacted by the government to regulate the appointment of people from lower socioeconomic classes to government jobs, unconstitutional, on the grounds that the government's power cannot be exercised in such a way as to deny reasonable equality of opportunity in matters of public employment to people from other socioeconomic classes.

<u>APPLICATION</u>

Due to the significance of the matter, the Supreme Court's Constitution Bench of five judges sent it to the Constitution Bench of nine judges to determine the final legal position on reservations. According to the ruling of the 6:3 majority, the Union Government's decision to provide SEBCs Creamy layer among them in 27% government employment was constitutionally valid.

Following were the significant proclamations:-

Creamy layer should not be allowed in the lower classes.

Article 16(4) allows for the classification of more backward classes as more backward classes.

Financial factors alone cannot accurately and fully distinguish a class of citizens who are behind.

A reservation shouldn't be more than 50%.

The Executive Order may be used to make reservations.

The promotion has no restrictions.

Permanent statutory body to investigate complaints of inclusion that is either too high or too low.

According to the majority, it is unnecessary to speak in on the Mandal Commission's work's accuracy or thoroughness.

The Supreme Court is the only forum for disputes involving new criteria.

<u>ANALYSIS</u>

The Mandal Commission relied on incredibly shoddy information. The surveys were only conducted in 0.06% of the villages, the committee itself acknowledged. Numerous castes were only included because the Kaka Kalelkar-led Backward Classes Commission's initial report made mention of them. The Kalelkar Commission and the State Government both designated a large number of castes as being historically underdeveloped.Even though the 1971 census was also available, the commission still used the 1931 and 1961 data to calculate the percentage of the lower classes. In doing so, they completely disregarded the demographic changes that have occurred over the past 50 years as well as the fact that Bangladesh, Pakistan, and Burma were all part of India in 1931.

Even though the 1971 census was also available, the commission still used the 1931 and 1961 data to calculate the percentage of the lower classes. In doing so, they completely disregarded the demographic changes that have occurred over the past 50 years as well as the fact that Bangladesh, Pakistan, and Burma were all part of India in 1931. Six out of nine judges accepted the report despite its catastrophic flaws, which included statistical errors, historical inaccuracies, and logical absurdities. The findings received harsh criticism from Justice Kuldip Singh, who stated: "A grouping of so-called backward castes by a clerical act based on drawing-room examination cannot be the backward classes intended under Article 16(4).

The Mandal Commission utilised "caste" as the sole basis to grant individuals reservation, disregarding all other factors, including economic background, and viewed "backward classes" and "backward castes" as synonyms. The commission disregarded the fundamental fact that it was only concerned with identifying the "behind class" for the sake of Article 16 and was not interested in the causes of social backwardness in Indian society (4). Since the Constitution employs the more general term "class" rather than "caste," Justice R.M. Sahai argued in his dissent that an interpretation that would identify backwardness on the basis of caste should be rejected.The goal and object of Article 16(2) would be destroyed if the State were given the authority to impose reservations under Article 16(4) based on religion, race, or caste, and this would violate the prohibition against caste-based discrimination.

The majority rejected the petitioner's argument that the level of reservation should be limited to 30%, which was the number mentioned in Dr. B.R. Ambedkar's speech before the Constitutional Assembly. The majority based their judgement on the quantum of reservation in State of Kerala v. N.M. Thomas. According to the majority, Article 16(4) was a feature of Article 16 and not an exception to 16(1).

CONCLUSION

The authors of the Indian Constitution opposed a casteless and provocative society. They pictured a society free of casteism, religious communalism, colour, place of residence, and language, and one that was homogenous, secular, and united.

The Indian Constitution acknowledges caste as one of the pertinent factors to be taken into account in the process of identifying persons who are socially backward, but it is neither caste-blind nor caste-biased. Reservations made primarily on the basis of caste would be against the law and could lead to cruel reverse discrimination. It is not acceptable to use the idea of equality to excuse further misconduct.

The court correctly held that the rank can be both regularly and social class for the key question of whether the grouping depends on standing or financial premise.

With regard to the second question, the court found that Article 16(4) is a free provision and not a particular situation under Article 16(1). Reservations may be made in accordance with condition (1) if a reasonable agreement is reached and the decision in Balaji v. Province of Mysore is disregarded.

The court concluded that Article 16(4) encompasses all other SC, ST, and other in backward class of citizens, including SEBCs, to a much greater extent. In response to the fourth concern, the court adequately defined this strategy and overturned the Balaji finding by holding that the distinction between backward classes and even more backward classes is valid. Sub-characterization is essential if backward classes are to fully benefitfrom reservation.

Among the classes who were given reservations, those who had previously profited from them and had raised their social standing (the "creamy layer") shouldn't be permitted to do so repeatedly. The lower classes should be given the opportunity to benefit from reservations in order to advance their status, not the upper class, who should refrain from exploiting them.

Although there was a little bit of an unusual cycle while handling this case, the court can also include the poor segment of high stations in SEBCs. The Supreme Court has made a strong effort to strike a balance between the interests of society and educationally in backward classes and a man having a place with the general classification in matters of government work.

CHAPTER TEN

THE SHIFT IN IMMIGRATION LAWS ACCROSS THE GLOBE

Author: Shreya Dubey, II year of B.A.,LL.B. from The Maharaja Sayajirao University of Baroda

INTRODUCTION

Approached by the carriers of both anguish and prosperity, Immigration has existed throughout the centuries. This global social movement has hence evolved and transitioned accordingly, with the age, time and places it has existed, and so has it's laws. This article shall unravel and illustrate the major shift in immigration laws of a few leading countries across the globe, and further outline it's impact it has on the nations.

Let us first understand the concept of immigration and laws synonymously. Immigration is the movement of people either collectively or individually, who take permanent residence in a foreign country. The Immigration laws are the laws that governs this entire system of migration of people in a country. These laws are made majorly considering the consequences of the people who would reside in the country after immigrating. A systematic operation to function and control the foreign incomings is necessary, it upholds both the principle of sovereignty of the nation, and simultaneously peacefully maintains a necessary procedure regulating the immense diversity of population and immigrants.

Immigration occurs due to numerous causes, such as education or economic pursuits, favouring enviromental factors, or internal conflict within their nations leading them to escape events like terrorism, persecution or human rights violations1. History has already been quiet conspicuous in flaunting the dramatic events that have contributed in altering immigration laws of several countries. However the idea that should be recognized here is that there is a cyclic creation of these events is what has vastly contributed in advancement of immigration laws across the globe.

THE COMMENCEMENT OF IMMIGRATION LAWS

Beginning with the the 19th Century from the world's most popular nation, the United States of America. Immigration litigation grew sedulously in the United States until it came to an abrupt end in World War 1, which could be inferred to be as a result of the utmost disarray and homesickness of those times, that perhaps aided the native lands in bringing the 'lost' and 'wandering' back home. Furthermore, The Immigration Act of 1924 of the United States, established an annual quota, fixed to be as 150,000 in 1929, creating the national origins system, administering it with the responsibility of characterizing immigration policy for the next 40 years. The quotas of the countries were articulated directly depending upon the comprehensive measure of that origins of people of that nation in 1920.

The quotas eventually drastically reduced the flow of immigrants from southeastern Europe in favour of the countries of northwestern Europe. This system was later abolished in 1965 in consideration of a predominantly first-come, first-served policy. Incultation of countries outside of western hemisphere was finally inaugurated, and an yearly structure of immigrant visas of approximate 170,000, with 20,000 was allowed to any one nation. This new policy revolutionised the entire archetype of immigration in the United States. This was beginning of a new era, the arrival of the non-Europeans now formed the new dominant immigrant- group. Asia, Latin America, the Caribbean, and the Middle East diversified the population of United States now more than ever2.

With time the world was becoming more compassionate towards refugees. In the 1980's and '90s immigration laws were evolved, granting amnesty to illegal aliens, raising admission limits, and creating a system for validating refugees. Proceeding further in the timeline, post World War 2, immigration was largely the result of refugee movement during the 1950s and 60s, a period that also began the reign of the freedom and sovereignty of the many colonized nations. The United Kingdom had then brought up the 1948 British Nationality Act which privileged the citizens in the former colonial territories of the Commonwealth the right of British nationality. Immigrants were majorly responsible in resucitating the European Infrastructure after World War 2, however they were also marginalised, leading up to the the isolation of ethnic groups and minority communities. Some states dealt with this social exclusion by limiting future immigration, whereas others approached it more-inclusively, as an incorporation of the miscallaneous cultures into one articulated understanding of citizenship. Sarah Parry of the Lecturer, School of Social and Political Science, University of Edinburgh hence concludes that "Immigration is therefore closely related to citizenship and the social and political rights to which citizens of a state are entitled"3.

THE ROUTE OF THE INDIAN IMMIGRATION LAWS

The Immigration laws of India too have had a quite a turbulent ride throughout it's record of the evolution. Foreigners Act, 1864, was the first enactment made for dealing with foreigners which specified for the numerous procedures such as expulsion of foreigners and their arrest, detention pending removal, and other explanation of required conducts for the same. The Imperial Legislative Assembly, during the second World War, implemented the Foreigners Act, 1940, under which the very crucial concept of "burden of proof" was introduced, of which Section 7 of the Act stated that a question of nationality of a person was their responsibility to prove that he was not a foreigner.

The Foreigners Act, 1946, by repealing the 1940 Act, was enhanced with greater powers to deal with all foreigners. Apart from appropriately providing the definition of a 'foreigner', it empowered the government to make various provisions for prohibiting, regulating or restricting the entry of foreigners into India. However the most significant concept that led such impeccable implementation of this law, was that the 'burden of proof' lies with the person, and not with the authorities. Moreover, this had also been praised by the ultimate judicial authority of India, the Supreme Court. In 1964, came the Foreigners (Tribunals) Order, which had the jurisdiction to decide whether a person is a foreigner within the ambit of the Foreigners Act, 1946. The tribunal, which has powers similar to those of a civil court, gives reasonable opportunity to the person alleged to be a foreigner to produce evidence in support of his case, before passing its order.

Then came the The Illegal Migrants (Determination by Tribunals) Act of 1983. This Act led the deterioration of the implementation of immigration laws. Failure to recognize the concept of "burden of proof" as imperative for prosperous implementation of immigration laws led to the downfall of as it put quite a burden on the authorities to prove illegality of the migrants. This brought back the Foreigners Tribunals constituted under the Foreigners

(Tribunals) Order, 19644.

This movement of people has leads to such a vast exchange of ideas, culture and knowledge, and thus inculcates a fresh breathe of perspective. However, these laws have also provided pillars of strength when mankind gasped for durability and unity in times of war. Mankind's constant progression as creators and destroyers is what has ultimately led to such developments of global immigration laws, and hence this paradoxical exuberance is what drives us towards evolution of the global immigration laws.

CHAPTER ELEVEN

HUMAN RIGHTS OF STREET CHILDREN - A SOCIO LEGAL ISSUE IN INDIA

Author: Aman Kumar, III year of B.A.,LL.B. from KIIT School of Law Bhubaneswar, Odisha.

Co-author: Divyanshu Raj, III year of B.A.,LL.B. from KIIT School of Law Bhubaneswar, Odisha.

First and foremost, before delving further into this topic, it is critical to understand the definition and scope of the term "street children." Street children is not a word, but rather a situation of those children who suffer from poverty as a result of homelessness, with the cause of homelessness being that they were abandoned by their parents due to poverty and were either left homeless or sold for exploitation. In general, these children live on the streets and feed themselves by performing challenging tasks in order to survive and live a life. Destitute children are those who are kicked out of the house by a single parent or are forced to leave their homes by a single parent in economically developed countries. Looking at the situation, we can conclude that this type of youngster is quite similar to street children in that they are also compelled to make a living on the street and are frequently abused, neglected by society, and, in the worst-case scenario, dead.

"Criminals are not born, they are made," goes an old adage that we've all heard at some point in our lives. As a result, we may claim that children are not born as street children, but are shaped as a result of society's carelessness. If we look at our own nation, India, the situation is even worse, as it is typical to witness children begging for money and other necessities or selling various types of things to make a meager living in locations like bus stops, main roadways, and train stations. One of the key issues is that street children become victims of criminal conduct as a result of their separation from mainstream society.

The United Nations Organization's Declaration of Human Rights was the first proper body to come to the aid of street children with some proper answers. The United Nations Human Rights Council established a framework to address the gravity of the social legal issue and set in place numerous measures to fight for the rights of this group. Part IV of the Indian Constitution's directive principles of state policies, as well as Part III of the Indian Constitution's fundamental

rights, provide for the protection of children, as well as the responsibility of both the central and state governments to take significant steps to promote the growth and development of these groups.

1.) THE SOCIETY AND STREET CHILDREN: To understand and appreciate the study of street children, you must first understand and admire the meaning and definition of the term Street children. To put it another way, street children are children who are poor (homeless) who live on the streets of a city begging for food. As previously stated, some children, referred to as destitute children or tossed out children, were forced to leave home due to single parents. Street children are young girls and boys of all ages who live and work in public locations in the vast majority of the world's cities. We can argue that street children are not born this way, but society is to blame for such heinous behavior. Everyone has seen women clutching newborns and begging for survival on bus stops, stations, traffic signals, and other public places. This is a sad reality, and it is not only in India, but also in western countries. We all know that determining the precise number of street children is extremely difficult, and that the figure is likely to be in the millions. As we all know, the world's population is rapidly increasing, and the number of street children is increasing as well. We should also keep in mind that not all street children are orphans, and that many of them keep in touch with such children's families while working on the streets to run their family's financial situation. Due to physical or sexual abuse, many street children have fled their homes. The unfortunate reality is that society does not treat street children well, since many of them are forced to engage in harmful behaviors and many are considered trash.

2.) SOCIO-LEGAL ISSUES: If we look at the term "street children," we can see that they exist all over the world. It has become a very essential component of society, and it is one of the factors obstructing the growth of street children's well-being. To understand the socio-legal issue, we must first understand what street children are: youngsters who have no home but the streets. Such children are thrown out of their homes or abandoned when they are born on the streets, and in order to live, they make the streets their homes and perform any kind of hard labor. The reasons why street children-humans work and live are as follows:

WHO has identified the reasons for street children being on the streets, including-

Neglected Children- These are the youngsters whose needs are not met as they grow up due to poverty, and as a result, they walk the streets to make a living. A neglected child is one who is found begging or without a home or parents, according to section 2(2) of India's Children Act 1960, and such children are examples of socio-legal issues that must be handled.

Unwanted Children- Each year, over a huge number of new born children in our country are thrown out because they are undesired, according to estimates. The child born in a broken household, by an unwed mother, or by a prostitute falls into this category, and children born from them are completely neglected because they have no standing and are looked down upon in society; such cases are socio-legal issues.

3.) CATEGORIES OF CHILD LABOUR: Child labour has had a negative impact on children's physical and mental development.

Street Children- As you can see in this paper, the location where street children can be discovered, and their situation is not the same as child labour. Children are guaranteed work and return home in the evening, just as they are in child labour, but street children are completely reliant on employees and live in bus stops, stations, and other public places, moving from place to place, and their predicament is more difficult than that of factory-worked children who live at home.

Forced Labor- In this situation, children are there because of their parents or because they are there for only one reason: they must pay off a debt inherited from their parents or themselves, and they must work under them to do so. Historically, this type of labor was associated with rural economies, in which peasants from economically disadvantaged communities were forced to work for landlords.

Children Used For Sexual Exploitation-Further investigation reveals that many young girls and boys satisfy the carnal desires of men from all walks of life. Sexual exploitation occurs most frequently in factories, workshops, bus stops, and railway stations, where youngsters labour. Children have little option but to be mistreated by their employers, and debts must be repaid through the labour of their daughters, making sexual exploitation one of the mass dangerous types of child labour.

4.) NON-GOVERNMENTAL ORGANIZATIONS (NGOs) AND THE MEDIA: Non-governmental organizations (NGO's) and the media have played an important role in raising awareness about this predicament. Creating a social climate in which street children are heard instead of oppressed. NGO briefings and interventions with relevant ministries and government on a regular basis. We are all aware that millions of children under the age of 18 live in India, representing a diverse range of cultures, faiths, castes, and socioeconomic groups. Several organizations are examining the status of street children around the world and working to improve it.

5.) LAW PROVISIONS RELATING TO STREET CHILDREN'S PROTECTION: As previously stated, the issue of street children and the preservation of their rights is a global concern, not just in India. According to Article 1 of the 1948 Universal Declaration of Human Rights, all humans are born free and equal in dignity and rights. As a result, all street children who are abandoned on the streets are born free and cannot be forced to labor or subjected to abuse that jeopardizes or damages their rights and dignity. According to Article 3, everyone, including street children, has the right to liberty and life, and as a result, they can live a normal life without hardship. No one shall be subjugated to slavery, as stated in article 4, and this trade will be forbidden in all enterprises. According to Article 26(1), everyone has the right to an education.

The Child Rights Information Network (C.R.I.N.) was established in 1983. It is a global coalition of 1600 non-governmental organizations (NGOs) advocating for the implementation of the United Nations Convention on the Rights of the Child. While all children need to be protected, some are more vulnerable than others and require special care due to social, economic, or geographical circumstances.

The Indian Constitution guarantees various rights to all children in India. The following are the Special and Guaranteed Articles:

Article 21.A: All children aged six (6) to fourteen (14) years get free and compulsory education from the state.

Article 24: states that not a single child who is below 14 years should be employed in any form of work.

Article 39(e): The state shall, in particular, direct its policies toward ensuring that workers', men's and women's, and children's, vulnerable ages are not misused, and that citizens are not driven by economic necessity to engage in avocations unsuited to their age or strength, and other related articles.

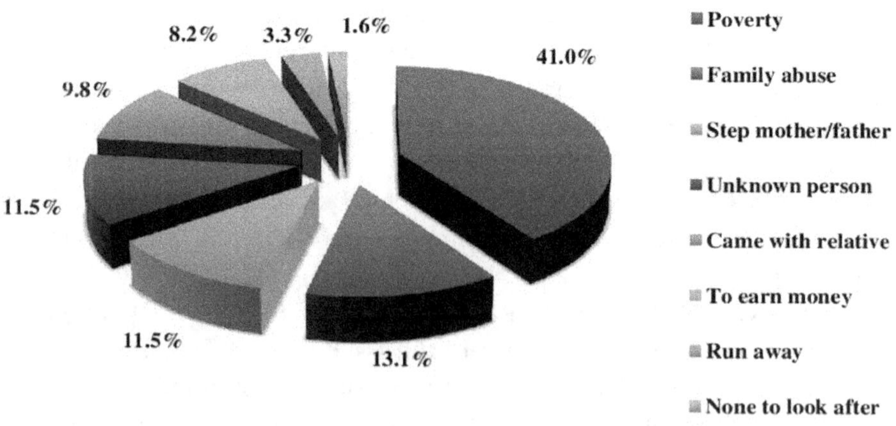

Graph representing the factors for becoming street children.

This study shows that street children, whether they are with their families or on their own, are especially vulnerable to the risks of society. Poverty is viewed as the fundamental cause of their existence on the streets. While the majority of the children lived under parental supervision and received some care and protection, they all encountered problems and challenges on a daily basis. The government should provide assistance to those non-governmental organizations (NGOs) that are working hard to help such youngsters get out of their predicament by providing them with food, shelter, and other necessities.

People should also be made aware of the problem that street children face so that society can come together and find a viable solution and offer assistance in any way possible. In this way, basic human rights can be preserved and will be of great benefit to these underprivileged children. Finally, because a child is a national asset, every citizen has a responsibility to protect them.

The source of social construction is assumed to be human interpretation. People understand the acts of others and how they form social relationships. The impressions and feelings of social workers cannot possibly be the same as those of a street youngster.They can provide a descriptive opinion regarding the differences in individual personality development and the causes that lead to the child being on the street from their perspective, but never a true one from the child's perspective. That is why it is critical to emphasize that this thesis is written from the perspective of a professional, not from the perspective of a single street child.

Our approach to street children, in my opinion, should be rights-based rather than welfare-based. It is critical to acknowledge that these children, like all children, have a fundamental right to protection, a safe environment, an education, and health care. An integrated and comprehensive programme (education, health, nutrition, and legal assistance) must be devised to overcome any economic, mental, or physical barriers they may have met at the regional level. A system must be put in place to provide education and health care to these youngsters while keeping their lifestyle in mind; a residential school where all of their needs are met while necessary safety precautions are taken could be an option. In addition, community awareness campaigns regarding economic and political rights are required, as are sensitization courses for police officers to better equip them to deal with these children.

CHAPTER TWELVE

CONCERN OF SOFTWARE OWNERSHIP FROM COPYRIGHT PERSPECTIVE

Author: Shraddha Sharma, B.A.,LL.B. from Sardar Patel Subharti Institute of law

INTRODUCTION

The introduction of the computer system ushered in a new era of technological innovation and has been largely responsible for the transformation of the technology and network sectors. Two operative platforms, the software and the hardware, run any computer. In layman's terms, we can say that the hardware is the tangible element while the software is the immaterial element. Both of these components are unique from one another in terms of any intellectual property that is awarded to them. Given that it mostly relates to physical things, such as computer systems or computer components like disc drives, memory chips, bus topologies, and monitors, such hardware frequently qualifies for protection under national patent laws.

SOFTWARE COPYRIGHT PROTECTION

The person who created the source code for the software or the author is generally considered to be the owner of the copyright to the software, which is protected by copyright laws. Copyright covers more than just ideas and facts; it also covers how they are communicated and presented in concrete form. Therefore, copyright protection is only given to the final tangible medium of expression that can be copied.

Because computer programmes were once thought of as immaterial objects, historically, computers and computer programmes were not given any such copyright protection.The laws governing copyright were further expanded to grant computer-readable software codes the same rights as "literary creations."

The term of "literary work" in the Copyright Act of 1957 covers computer programmes, tables, compilations, and computer databases. The categories of works in which the copyright is granted are outlined in Section 13 of the Act, and this list includes original literary works.

Computer software that does not have a technological effect is protected by copyright law, according to the Indian Copyright Act of 1957. Computer software must be original in order to be granted copyright protection, and it must also have been created with enough skill and effort to demonstrate that it is original.

<u>COPYRIGHT AND THE STAFF AND CONTRACTORS OF DEVELOPING COMPANY</u>

As was said above, copyright does not necessitate a formal registration in order to acquire the IP right over the work, in contrast to other IP rights like patents, trademarks, etc. Although formal copyright registration offers benefits for demonstrating IP rights in court during disputes, infringements, etc. As a result, the author acquires the copyright to the work upon its creation.

There are two groups of employees—or people—who assist in the creation of software or in the provision of services in a software development company, or in any other business.

The other group of employees consists of freelancers or contractors who are hired to perform a specific or specialised service. Upon completion of that service, the freelancers or contractors are qualified to receive a specific payment from the business, and their employment relationship with the latter ends. A section pertaining to the IP assignment in the contract that the company engages into with both of these groups of people clarifies who owns the IP right when they provide services to the firm.

Any intellectual property developed by employees would typically belong to their employers. With the employee, a different contract for the assignment of IP may be made.

The software or other products that employees produce are regarded as being work produced for payment. As a result, at the time of creation, employers have ownership. To ensure that no intellectual property (IP) belongs to the employee for any creations, the IP assignment clause in the contract has been carefully designed.

Even if an employee writes the software code for a firm that develops software, the copyright for that work would still belong to the employer or the business. However, it would be intriguing to comprehend a scenario in which such a person wrote software during his formal working hours for the organisation he is engaged with.

In such a situation, a business or the employer might have a claim on the software if it is related to the sector or range of services the firm provides, or if it falls within the purview of his employment. A business may decide to hire independent contractors or vendors to carry out tasks for them or even to create software specifically for the business. In such a situation, it is usually preferable to protect the firm's intellectual property rights by entering into a work-for-hire agreement with such freelancers and having the freelancers transfer any ownership rights over the work they particularly made for the company to the company itself.

The onus is on the business to be aware of this and make sure that such a contract is made with the independent contractors. In the United States, unless a contract clearly states otherwise, there is no requirement that any job produced by a freelancer would result in a work for hire. Therefore, it becomes crucial for any business working with freelancers, vendors, or contractors to sign a separate contract transferring IP rights ownership to the business.

<u>WHEN YOU SHOULD DISCUSS COPYRIGHT WITH YOUR DEVELOPMENT TEAM ?</u>

Discussing who should own the copyright from the very beginning would be the wisest course of action in both parties' best interests. An internal software development team ought to have an IP assignment clause in their employment contract since they should ideally be made up of company workers. However, the employer should make sure an IP assignment agreement is reached with the development team if they have not already agreed upon such a condition. Once the programme development is complete, this assignment and ownership of the copyright will take place. Also significant is the requirement that such an agreement specifically specify that the work was "work-made-for-hire." Developers must negotiate a licence to the software in the same manner that third parties would if they want to have any right to use it in the future or for various projects. A clause identifying the code as a work-made-for-hire, assigning the code to the client upon completion, or granting the customer a licence to use the code upon completion will therefore be present in any well-written software development contract.

THINGS TO THINK ABOUT BEFORE WORKING WITH A SOFTWARE DEVELOPMENT BUSINESS

Over time, it has been noted that the largest software development organisations have begun working with outside software development teams to create or create software for them. These businesses see a variety of management and technical advantages in contracting out the work to outside contractors. However, these advantages also invited a few legal issues that the market actors had previously disregarded. In order to avoid these legal repercussions, it is necessary for any firm intending to hire an outside party to create software for them to have a specific checklist. Some of these factors that need to be looked into before or during contracting a vendor have been listed by us.

a. Contractual

The management must select whether or not to get into a formal contract with the external party, which is one of the most crucial factors. By establishing a written contract, you would provide the groundwork for all the other things to come and help to ensure that some crucial details are recorded and not lost in a verbal debate.

b. Possession

Understanding and choosing who is entitled to ownership of the software and intellectual property rights becomes extremely important, as was explained in the article above. Both sides should talk about and bring up the issue of who will own the technology. However, it's possible that some unique background or pre-existing IPs of these vendors won't be transferred to the business because they are clearly their property.

The decision of who will be the owner and any associated limitations are simply one part of the ownership element. Such third-party suppliers may be prohibited from disclosing to any other third parties and from subcontracting to others, among other restrictions.

c. Intellectual property management

The argument for IP ownership may also include this issue, but it is equally important to choose who will oversee the management of the IP and assure its security. This should ideally belong to the owner. However, the business may decide to speak with and solicit feedback from the software vendor.

d. Process administration

From a strictly business perspective, certain requirements for the development, its acceptance criteria, the creation of a beta version, the incorporation of updates, delivery timeframes, etc., must be met. Understanding and include such clauses in a contract that correctly reflects the demands and requirements of the service recipient is always in their best interests.

e. Liabilities and infringement indemnity

When an external software development team is hired to conduct the services, a clause regarding responsibilities and indemnity against any violation of third-party intellectual property becomes necessary. The question of whether we, as service recipients, are entitled to such indemnities and if they are enforceable in a court of law needs to be brought up.

f. Discontinuation

Last but not least, the termination of the contract is a crucial component of every agreement. The right to termination and the repercussions of termination must be specified in the contract's section on termination.

CONCLUSION

Many businesses in the US and other countries have used using external suppliers or software developers as a strategic tool. The aforementioned guidelines for completing due diligence should be taken into account if one is prepared to choose an external software development team. One should also be aware of the implications of doing so. To understand the role of IP in the software, it is, nevertheless, all the more crucial to look into the features of IP rights with a lawyer or IP specialist.

CHAPTER THIRTEEN

MERGER IN THE INDIAN SKIES

Author: Zaier Ahmad, III year of B.A. LL.B (Hons.) from National Law Institute University, Bhopal

Co-author: Adnan Danish, III year of B.A. LL.B (Hons.) from National Law Institute University, Bhopal

Introduction

Indian giant whose business expands from salt to steel, the Tata Conglomerate made a recent announcement that it is planning to consolidate the entire airline business by 2024 which will be under a single brand- Air India. Cherishing the dream of their forerunner, an aviator, Industrialist and Chairman of Tata Group J.R.D. Tata, Tata Sons, via its fully subsidiary Talace Private Investment("Talace") on 27th January,2022 acquired Air India from the Indian Government.

Who are the Stakeholders in the Merger

Currently, the Indian Behemoth owns a total of four airlines, including a 100% ownership in Air India and its subsidiary India Express, 83.67% in Air-Asia, 51% in Vistara, and rest 49% in Vistara controlled by Singapore Airlines Limited (SIA).

After the aforementioned consolidation, which is anticipated to take place in the year 2024, Tata will hold 74.9% of the new company, Singapore Airlines Limited will hold 25.1%, and as part of the agreement, SIA will invest Rs. 2,059 crores in Air India.

Objective of the Merger

At the very outset, the first process will be the consolidation of Air India and Air Asia within a year, and then finally it will conclude with the Consolidation of Vistara into Air India.The principal cause for this is that Air India wants to expand its network, revive its Maharaja Air India image, and take market share away from Indigo and other international airlines.

Air India is concentrating on expanding both its network/coverage and aircraft fleet, overhauling its service offering, and improving safety, reliability, and consistency in performance as part of the transition to becoming a truly world-class airline. Building a strong Air India with full service and cheap service on both domestic and international flights is yet another ambition for Tata's.

Regulatory Approvals Involved in M&A transaction in Aviation Sector

M&A process in the aviation sector is more prone to government approval, authentication and authorization.It has to follow the regular procedure of Merger and Amalgamation as provided under Section 230-232 of the Companies Act,2013 additionally if there is any foreign direct investment it needs to fall in line with FDI Policy and NDI Rules, approval from the ministry of corporate affairs and other ministries if required. Finally, approval from the principal regulating authority under the Ministry of Civil Aviation is warranted.

Now, elucidating the process of M&A in the Aviation Sector, after the scheme is approved under the Companies Act and by the Ministry of Corporate Affairs,the role of CCI comes into play.

CCI Role in Merger in Aviation Sector: The Competition Act 2002 is the principal statute that governs the anti-trust framework in India. The Act does not particularly deal with or govern the airline sector, nonetheless, every notifiable combination has to pass through the provisions of the statute.

Section 3[i]of the Act provides that no enterprise or person or association of the above two shall enter into an agreement that can potentially have an appreciable adverse effect on competition in India. Further,Section 5[ii] provides that any combination exceeding the specified threshold shall have to be notified to CCI and such combination cannot be effectuated until the approval of CCI or 210 days have passed subsequent to the notification to CCI.[iii]

With this consolidation, the Air India group has the second-largest domestic market share of 25.9% behind only IndiGo,[iv] which could raise the eyebrows of the competition watchdog thereby warranting scrutiny.

The CCI implements the point of origin/point of destination (O&D) pair technique,[v]which is widely used internationally. According to this approach, every combination of a point of origin and a point of destination should be regarded to be a separate market from the customer's viewpointand CCI may apply conditions for authorisation if it believes that there are concerns about competition.In contrast, if there are no other viable options and there is a significant amount of network overlap with relatively low economic gains relative to the harm to competition, prohibiting the transaction may be the only recourse.

It's intriguing to note that since the CCI's formation, there have been around 850 filings submitted with the competition watchdog about issues connected to competition. It is noteworthy that despite 40 submissions undergoing revisions in order to be approved for Phase I and Phase II of review, no such combination has been prohibited or blocked.

By taking a quick look at the precedents, it is reasonable to assume that the competition watchdog would approve the merger of the two airlines. The Foreign Investment Promotion Board must be contacted for clearance if there is any foreign investment. Foreign airlines may invest up to 49% of the paid-up share capital through the automatic method and up to 100% through the government route in the air transport industry for passenger services. Such investments shall be subject to being scanned under the government approval route.

In the Air India and Vistara merger, Singapore Airlines which is a foreign entity investing via FDI will get a 25.1% stake in the merged entity,[vi] which is within the specified threshold.

Also, it is necessary to get security clearance of the Directors and the Chairman of the company, then the Acquiring company will first file No-Objection Certificate(NOC), this application needshould be submitted to the Ministry of Civil Aviation in a prescribed procedure along with requisite fee, when the scrutiny is completed by MoCA,[vii] the applicant who fills the basic criteria, the Directorate General of Civil Aviation(DGCA) issues initial NOC, the functions of DGCA is primary in nature as it enforces civil aviation regulations, all the standards which includes air safety and airworthiness standards, also it coordinates with International Civil Aviation Organisation,[viii] clearance related to use of Airport and other ground infrastructure facilities need to be obtained from Airport Authority of India(AAI). The appraisal of fees for passenger services and aeronautical services allows for the monitoring of performance standards in areas such as service quality, continuity, and dependability. Further, The Bureau of Civil Aviation Security (BCAS) is also responsible for determining security standards and is required to adhere to those set forth in national and international air safety treaties to which India is a signatory.

The relevant Act the scheme should satisfy in relation to Civil Aviation are: The Aircraft Act,1934, The Aircraft Rules 1937, The Air Corporations (Transfer of Undertaking and Repeal Act, 1994, The Carriage by Air Act,1972, The Civil Aviation Policy and The Civil Aviation Requirements.

<u>Critical Analysis</u>

Financial Analysis

When we assess the purpose and goals of mergers and acquisitions in the Indian airline industry, we find that the primary goal of the acquirer has always been to capture market shares of the target company; the aim of the company has not been to create a big entity and mutually share each other abilities to expand overseas and create an all-famous Indian Airline which works internationally well like Qatar Airways, Etihad Airways and Emirates.

The operational and financial Highlight of Indian Airlines after the merger is not quite impressive. In the case of Kingfisher and Air Deccan, the net profit of kingfisher during 2007-2008 was -188.14 Crores, after the merger, during 2012-13 the loss got widened and reached to -2328 Crores. When talking about Air India and Air Asia merger, the merger commenced in 2014, the financial health of Air Asia deteriorated more after its merger with Air Asia, the net profit in 2018 was -125.4 Crores and in 2022 it slipped to -2178 Crores.[ix] The track record with respect to financial health post-merger has not been pleasant in Indian Aviation Market.

Legal Analysis

When talking about past challenges in the M&A with respect to Civil Aviation, the Jet Airway and Air Sahara acquisition faced challenges related to the lack of aviation merger and acquisition that prevailed in India, situations like airport infrastructure transfer and uncertainty related to international route.

In the case study of Jet Airways and Etihad Airways in 2013, Jet Airways was on the verge of collapsewhen they were salvaged by Etihad.The merger had to face various investigation by the Department of Industrial Policy and Promotion, Ministry of Corporate Affairs, Department of Economic Affairs and Ministry of Civil Aviation, the transaction was also scrutinized by Competition Commission of India (CCI), SEBI and Foreign Investment Promotion Board (FIPB).

The Scheme of Arrangement between Deccan Aviation and Kingfisher but the scheme did not bear any fruit and both companies entwined into a legal battle about the lease agreement executed by both the parties, the Court had to step into the scheme of arrangement agreed by both the parties that is the Deccan Aviation and G.E Commercial Aviation Service. The court held that the supervision of lease agreement has nothing to do with the scheme of arrangement, if there exist an arrangement between the parties elsewhere with a competent authority and or a before an appropriate Court, without following the procedure it can't invoke the scheme of arrangement under 392 of Companies Act,1956.[x]

Air India and Indian Airlines merger also faced some issues like inconsistent administration, compensation discrepancies, employee unrest which hampered operations of the airline.

Conclusion

Merger and Acquisition in Aviation Industry is still an unexplored sector however with the boom in the market in general, M&A in the aviation sector will be on a rise. Looking at the precedents, arrangement/combination in the aviation sector is a risky scenario wherein the companies are not able to recover losses and any arrangement warrants a pre-planned objective and a mode of execution. The process is riddled with regulatory approvals thereby making it highly complex.

Subject to regulatory approvals the Air India merger is expected to be completed by 2024. The merged entity plans to increase its domestic market share to 30% in 5 years and significantly increase its international routes. With Indigo already holding 56% of the market share, the Indian Aviation market is moving towards a duopoly, a duopoly in Indian Sky.

CHAPTER FOURTEEN

DECRIMINALIZATION OF HOMOSEXUALITY IN INDIA

Author: Manaswini. Medepudi, IV year of B.B.A.,LL.B.(Hons.) from ICFAI Law School, Hyderabad, India.

INTRODUCTION

Homosexuality[i] is defined as the interactions involving people of the same sex. Across numerous families and communities, homosexuality has been historically regarded and widely ridiculed as deviant or abnormal based on philosophical, religious, and theological beliefs about what activities conform to reality and natural law.

LGBTQ - Lesbian, homosexual, bisexual, and transgender persons encounter identical and distinctive issues in human rights. LGBT and intersex (those born with abnormal anatomical traits) experience some of the same discriminations. Additionally, they experience institutional violence inside healthcare institutions, which has a long-lasting negative impact on their physical and mental well-being. These people encounter both common and unique obstacles in the context of human rights.

PROMINENT SOURCES – DEPICTION

Khajuraho Temple[ii], a notable temple in Madhya Pradesh, was adorned in antiquity featuring various statues representing sexuality. This had been constructed in the 10th Century by Rajput Chandela Dynasty kings. There is hardly any such temple in India that depicts humanity's emotions. Several sculptures show homosexual acts, demonstrating that homosexuality existed in the ancient epoch.

Manusmriti, a main body of legislation followed during that era by an overwhelming percentage of people, is remarkable. It urges that everyone who engages in homosexual behavior, either men or women,be encouraged to be punished. Although the script did not promote homosexuality at the time, it still did show that homosexuality existed.

The 1861 colonial-era norms and law regarding the homosexual element have finally been transformed by the 5 Judge bench, which has considered the modern societal culture and standards of the 21st Century. LGBTQ stands for Lesbian, gay, bisexual, transgender, or queer.

CHRONICLE OF HOMOSEXUALITY

The judicial request to decriminalize homosexuality was made in 1994 by the AIDS Bhedbhav Virodhi Andolan (ABVA)[iii]. However, it was denied by the Delhi High Court. The Naz Foundation then presented a similar legal petition to the Delhi High Court in 2001, which was again dismissed.

On July 2, 2009, the same Delhi High Court struck down parts of the clause as unlawful eight years later. Justice A.P. Shah handed down the landmark decision, the Delhi High Court's Chief Justice, and Justice S. Muralidhar at the time. Section 377 of the IPC was upheld unconstitutional by the Delhi High Court in NAZ Foundation v. N.C.T. of Delhi (2009)[iv].

The decision was also questioned in Suresh Kumar Kaushal v. NAZ Foundation (2014)[v][vi]before the Indian Supreme Court (SC), where it had reversed by a two-judge bench. In Navtej Singh Johar v. UOI[vii], a five-judge SC panel heard a new challenge to the SC ruling in 2016. In this case, a dancer and member of the LGBTQ community, Navtej Singh Johar,filed a petition under Article 32 of the Indian Constitution before the Supreme Court. This judgment symbolizes a revolutionary age of individual freedom and represents a significant triumph for the lesbian, homosexual, bisexual, and transgender movement, which has long determinedly campaigned for the legalization of gay sex.

LEGAL PROVISIONS AND DECRIMINALIZATION

Section 377 of the Indian Penal Code[viii], criminalized homosexuality and was established in 1861 under British regulation over India. Referred to as "unnatural offenses," and states that anybody who willingly engages in sexual contact with a man, woman, or animal in violation of nature's order shall be punished with life in jail.

Therefore, the Supreme Court of India decriminalized Section 377 of the IPC on September 6, 2018, allowing homosexual intercourse between consenting adults in a personal location. According to the Supreme Court, consenting adults to homosexual intercourse does not constitute an offense because sexual preference is innate, and individuals have no control over it.

EXPLANATION

The Court emphasized that Section 377 indiscriminately penalized those who indulge in same-sex relationships. To support this, the Court pointed out that Section 377 designates and punishes those who engage in carnal intercourse beyond the order of nature in a manner that protects women and children. This goal, however, has no apparent connection to the categorization because unnatural offenses are also separately penalized under Section 375 and the POCSO Act. As a result, the Court ruled that discriminatory treatment of LGBT people breaches Article 14.

Section 292 of the Indian Penal Code outlines obscenity, and today it empowers more than adequate space for the acceptance of homosexuality to fall within its purview.

The Indian Penal Code's Section 294, which punishes "obscene behavior in public," also pertains to and is used to prosecute homosexual men. Although the Protection of Children from Sexual Offences Act 2012 in England lessened the punishment for homosexual behavior with consensual sex, consent is primarily irrelevant in India for forming an offense as specified under this clause.

PRESENT SCENARIO AND SUGGESTIONS

Homosexuality is immutable and inborn in nature. The acts of violence and discrimination against homosexuals are creating a negative impact, although there has been a green flag from the judiciary. The state has to plan to improvise and implement the laws to forbid discrimination against a homosexual based on sexual orientation and gender identity.

Thus be awareness programs to educate people about LGBTQI rights and sexual orientation and not limit their liberty of being as accessible as others. The Supreme Court of India has legalized consenting homosexual con regarding gay marriage. As everyone has the freedom to select their life partner without any discrimination, not even based on gender. The law must adapt as society does. The law needs to adapt to the culture. The legislation does not specify the legal status of same-sex unions in India.

By applying penalties under any legislative decree, it hasn't discriminated against same-sex weddings. The moment has come for legislationnot to discriminate against homosexuals.

The critical legal responsibilities of States in safeguarding the human dignity of LGBT individuals should comprise the mentioned:

- Defend them against abuse that is homophobic and transphobic.
- Stop practicing violence and other inhumane or brutal methods

- Abrogate the laws that make same-sex relationships and transgender individuals illegal
- Against grounds of discrimination on sexual orientation born trait status
- Protect the rights to free speech, association, and assembling in peace for LGBTI persons.

These would make the world a better and more pleasant place to live in.

<u>Author's Bio</u>

Manaswini Medepudi is a fourth-year undergraduate student of law [B.B.A., L.L.B(Hons.)] at ICFAI Law School, Hyderabad, India. Her areas of interest in law include Aviation, Maritime, TMT, and Corporate Law. And She is upskilling herself to pursue her higher education abroad soon.

CRAVATH MODEL IN THE INDIAN LEGAL PROFESSION

Author: Sharvari Yadnesh Sambhus, LL.M from Jindal University

The legal System in India and particularly the Indian legal profession has changed, even though not drastically, but has somewhat changed in the past few decades. Be it from mergers to international law, the profession has become more prominent due to globalization. Also,in my opinion, the base of success achieved by any law firm is the associates they hire, what those associates acquire in the future.A good metaphor for the same would be, the young generation is the future of any nation, likewise, the basic hiring or the associates decide the future of a specific firm. But does that mean that only the ones in the big law schools isthe only chance of getting partnership at a big law firm? According to the Cravath Model, in my opinion, there were majorly nine features of hiring. But before that, let us see some history behind the Cravath Model, ages ago, the law-firm in New York, Cravath Swaine & Moore LLP had a partner named Paul Cravath who invented the Cravath System.

This system was basically a set of principles or features which was a foundation used for hiring. It was a system which, on the right path, evolves to success.

The essential features of the old Cravath Model were:

- Hiring the best legal graduates from the best law schools at the best salaries.
- Rigorous training alongside of the partners, so they could work on cases as well as be observed.

Permanent employment was given only to the partners. Where associates were observed to be of a greater value, they would keep them otherwise rest others were let loose.

The equity ownership of the firm was under a tight control.

The very old Cravath model used to offer the associates nothing, it was dependent on what the associates could bring into the firm, later Cravath was supposed to be the first one to hire the associates by giving them salaries.

The partners would be promoted only on the basis of the office.

The firm did not take any political favours so as to stay outside the loophole and avoid the curve ball.

The firm believed in an executive decision. Like a senior partner or so.

The clients were charged according to an hourly rate.

This model worked very well, as there was nothing pertaining to any harm of the firm, it worked well for the best firms, who supported the theory. According to Cravath model, hiring the best associates, was the first step, like graduates from the best colleges, editors, people who were keen to the knowledge and who could quickly grasp the system. Many factors contributed to the success of the Cravath System, but one key factor was how well the firms internalized the system's core elements.[1]

In around 2000's, the legal industry started to experience significant changes. The changes included these included the rise of competition and the increasing number of clients and professionals wanting more. The modern legal industry is now more focused on providing a variety of options and a better work environment.

The end of the Cravath Model may bring a halt to the legal industries traditions of mutual respect and accountability. However, these changes do not break the industries of today's elite professionals.

One of the Cravath Model's core principles is the belief that lawyers should have a deep working knowledge of multiple practice areas. During the early twentieth century, most firms were only focused on one or two lawyers. As the industrial revolution began to take hold, Paul Cravath recognized the need for law firms to evolve their approach.

He focused on hiring the best graduates from the best law schools and developing them as generalists so they can create a team with shared values. He also sought out candidates with passion skilled associates would eventually become partners, but only after having been well-versed in the firm's various facets.

The new Cravath model encouraged partners to not compete with one another for business credit or hold their own book of business. All clients would get the best advice regardless of who their key partner was. Paul Cravath established the value system that we still use today. It helped define a new model for American firms for the profession and a desire to work hard.

Upon joining a Firm, according to the Cravath Model, the associates were rotated to another group to learn various disciplines. Until very recently, most deep-pocketed companies of Big Law were only able to access top-quality legal talent and resources through their corporate clients. This has caused many of them to turn to do-it-yourself solutions or rely on unlicensed legal advice. The rapid emergence and evolution of new business models in the legal industry has greatly expanded the variety of low-cost legal services on the market. Disruptive innovation is a phenomenon that occurs when a small company can compete with established businesses by offering lower prices and better products or services. As the entry continues to improve its offerings, its customer base continues to expand. This is when the entry becomes the dominant player in the market.

On a broad level, with globalization coming into existence, in my opinion, the Cravath model has pushed the Indian legal profession into a brighter future. All in all, the development in the Cravath Model has been an inclination along with globalization, it has been a real boost for the Indian Legal Profession as well as the legal system in India.

CHAPTER SIXTEEN

DOMESTIC VIOLENCE AGAINST MEN IN INDIA

Author: Reethamshi Kolipaka, IV year of B.B.A.,LL.B.(Hons.) from ICFAI Law School, Hyderabad.

In recent times, women are also earning, self-sufficient, and aware of their rights due to globalization and westernization. There is a structural change in the families due to socioeconomic conditions in society which is enabling women to recognize that they are not inferior to men.

The term "Domestic Violence" includes a broad range of violent acts committed by one member of a family or household against another[i]. It often refers to the mistreatment of a child or spouse, and includes not only physical harm but also threats and verbal, psychological, and sexual abuse.

Domestic abuse, also called "Domestic violence" or "intimate partner violence," is defined by the United Nations[ii] as a pattern of behaviour designed to establish or retain power and control over an intimate partner in any relationship. Abuse is defined as physical, sexual, emotional, financial, or psychological acts or threats against another individual. The relationship between the perpetrator and the victim is the crucial to the distinction between assault charges and domestic violence.

Domestic violence against women is well recognized by law in India. But the domestic violence against men is an issue that is never taken seriously. It is not recognized as a crime by Indian law. The laws against domestic violence in India are women centric and excludes the possibility that men can also be harassed by women.

As per Section 498A[iii] of the Indian Penal Code, 1860 only husband or relative of husband of woman can subject a woman to cruelty. Further it reads as "Whoever, being the husband or the relative of the husband of a woman, subjects such woman to cruelty shall be punished with imprisonment for a term which may extend to three years and shall also be liable to fine." But there is no further provision which makes woman liable for spousal violence.

Section 3[iv] of the Protection of Women Domestic Violence Act, 2005 protects only women against domestic violence. But there is no such provision that shelters the men from the same violence.

Domestic Violence can be in the form of physically, mentally, emotionally, and psychologically affecting a person's life in every way. As per the recent study by Malik and Nadda[v], emotional abuse is found to be the most common spousal violence followed by physical abuse.

Physical abuse includes slapping, pushing, hitting by spouse or their relatives, throwing objects at the spouse.

Mental abuse includes threatening to expose personal information to others, showing oppressive possessiveness or jealousy or threatening to harm themselves, forcing him to send his parents to old age home, Financial abuse includes taking all the earnings of the husband or giving allowance from his own earnings and refusing him to support his parents financially.

Psychological abuse also a form of mental violence includes criticizing the husband, name calling and using berating language; threatening or giving constant threats under false allegations of dowry and domestic violence. But all these forms of abuse against men goes unreported.

Lack of education, earning lesser income, one spouse earning higher income, unemployment, addiction, etc. are some of the major reasons of domestic violence against men in India.

The main issue in Indian society with domestic violence is that it is taken seriously once in a while. If it happens with women, it is ignored as something that women have to face because of gender and if it happens with men, it is considered unreasonable and illogical. We have to create an equal society where the spousal violence is wrong irrespective what the perpetrator's gender is as any type of violence is gross violation of human rights.

Domestic violence cases against men in India goes unreported because of the following factors

General stereotypes about men that they are strong and they are the protectors of the family. Fear of false cases against them and their family by women if they disclose or report the violence as the laws in India are gender specific. Fear of losing the custody of children due to the legal battle between them and their partner. Denial that domestic violence can only happen against women is one of the major factor for the under reporting the cases of domestic violence by men. Another main factor is labelling men as cowards, girlish and others when they try to expose their vulnerabilities.

As per NCRB Suicide Report, 2020[vi]total suicides in country were 153, 052 in which male suicides amount to 108,532 (70.9%) out of which 73, 093 were married men. It also reveals that suicide among men after marriage is rising and rising. This mainly due to the abuse they face in one or the other form from their intimate partner. And also lack of laws protecting the rights of men in case of violation of their human rights i.e. domestic violence against them by their intimate partner.

In conclusion, Human rights and gender equality belongs to both men and women. The term 'Domestic Violence' nowhere indicates that only women can be the victim of domestic violence, men can also be the victim and not only perpetrator. A victim of domestic violence is a victim irrespective of the gender of the perpetrator. Domestic violence should be now classified as spousal violence or intimate partner violence as men can also be the victim of the same. Along with legislations there is a need for the society to repudiate the idea of patriarchy and start to normalize men being sensitive and emotional.

It's high time for the laws to be gender neutral. Apart from the absence of the law, societal norms also stop men from seeking justice. Patriarchy makes it appear that men can never face violence and this notion towards men make the victims and society to ignore or be silent about their sufferings. Being beaten up by a woman is perceived as a challenge to one's masculinity. The patriarchal society which gives a man the power to subjugate a woman actually subverts his ability to call for help when faced with domestic violence.

CHAPTER SEVENTEEN

ETHICAL DIMENSIONS BEHIND DRAUPADI'S CHEER-HARAN

Author: Asmita Srivastava, II year of B.B.A.,LL.B. from Symbiosis Law School

Mahabharata is an epic written by Ved-vyas, telling the story of the throne of the Hastinapur and the dynastic conflict behind this throne. This story has everything a modern- day thriller contains and lot more. Every time one reads this great epic, there is always something new to discover in here. No character is flawless or divided between black and white. All the characters have their strengths and flaws and their respective grey shade. There are many lessons hidden everywhere and for everyone in this story. One of the greatest lesson this epic teaches is the one of Karma. This epic has something for everyone.

Draupadi's Cheer-haran was that one event that changed the course of history. A dice game gone wrong, and a woman paid the price. She was dishonoured and insulted in one of the most prestigious courtsof that era. Why was the court silent? why were the husbands of this woman silently looking at everything that was happening? Why was this not stopped?

This event of history has always been under the lens of the people of anyone that has remote knowledge of Mahabharata. People of all generations have asked questions that very are similar to the ones that I asked earlier. In this essay, I would like to analyze the moral dimensions and ethical dilemma that filled the court that unfortunate day.

This all started when the Pandavs were ruling Indraprasth and one day Duryodhan invited them for a game of dice. Duryodhan and Shakuni (his maternal uncle) trapped the brothers into betting their empire, wealth and then themselves as well. Shakuni was a master at the game of dice and the dice that he played with was made of this father's bones, which meant that the dice would always play in the favour of Shakuni. After this, Shakuni suggested them to put their wife, Draupadi to wager everything they lost in the gameand Yudhishthira plays into the ploy of Shakuni and stakes Draupadi in the game and losses her as well.

After losing everything they ever owned in the game of dice, they were in line to watch the greatest tragedy in the story, the Cheer-haran of Draupadi. As soon as they lost the bet, Duryodhan orders her to the join court, when she doesn't return after her first call. Dushasana goes to bring her to the court. Dushasana slaps her then drags her to the court with her hair. And then after the order of Duryodhan, he starts to disrobe her in the presence of the whole court. Seeing that all her husbands are helpless, she starts praying to Lord Krishana to save her from this travesty. And Krishana listens to her prayers and adds on lines and lines of clothes into her garment, while Dushasanakeeps trying to reach the end of it. This goes on for quite some time when he tires himself and gives up.

When all this comes to a stop, a grief stricken Draupadi curses the whole court to their deaths. She also decides not to tie her hair till she washes it with the blood of her molester, Dushasana while Bhīma pledges to drink his blood as revenge and break the lap of Duryodhan, the one he offered to her to sit on. And thus the clock for the War of Kurukshetra began ticking.

Yudhishthira, the eldest of the Pandav Brothers. The son of Yama: God of Dharma and Death.He was master in spear-fighting and chariot racing. Yudhishthira was a polyglot, knowing unusual languages. He was known for his honesty, justice, sagacity, tolerance, good behaviour and discernment[1]. The most respected man in Pandavs and someone who is idealised by a lot of people but the flaws of his character were on display during this event.

From the beginning of the gamble the Pandavs were doomed, they were a lot of things that Yudhishthira could have avoided. He gambled his empire, his wealth and himself but he had no right to gamble his brothers or his wife. It was his moral responsibility to keep his brothers and his wife safe. And his silence put huge question marks on his ethical character.

How did his principles allow him to stay put, while his wife was being disrobed in public and was able to remain silent? The ethical dilemma between being someone's slave and a husband put him in position where silence seemed like the best option, but was it?

A king gambling his kingdom, a brother gambling his brothers and a husband gambling his wife, no dharma allows these sins. The man that had upheld dharma on his shoulder, fell to his knees with a simple game of dice. To a limit all the deeds of his could be justified, but under no circumstance can his silence during the 'Cheer-haran' can be seen as anything but an act of cowardice. According to the ethics, he was supposed to stand up for his wife. He should have stopped Dushasana from dragging his wife into to the court, or Duryondhana asking her to sit on his laps or disrobing her but he put his head down and did nothing. Just because he was enslaved, doesn't mean he had no right to protect her. If had the right to gamble her off, then it was his moral responsibility to protect her from the consequences of his action.

And all these accusations are not limited to the eldest Pandav. None of the brothers, tried to stop their elder brother from gambling everything away. Bhīma, the son of the Vayu; Arujan, the son of Indra and Nakul and Sahdev, the sons of Ashwini brothers; all of them masters of different arts, wise and were upholders of dharma like their brother. So, why were they silent when their empire and wealth was getting gambled away. Why did none of the brothers think it was their moral and ethical responsibility to stir their brother away from the part of destruction?

Their silence and helplessness was all the made-up in their mind. All it takes is one voice of reason, before a destruction to save everything. Ethically, as the guardians of a kingdom, the safety and the well-fare of the people in their kingdom was their responsibility, and to silently let it be handed-over in a game of dice, doesn't account for Dharma or gambling away their wife.

Yudhishthira should not be blamed alone, he was just the voice but due the silence all of brothers they are considered as an active participant and are the equal shareholder of the blame.

Next-in-line would be the godfather of the Throne of Hastinapur; Bhishma. The man with skills of a god, wisdom of the world, spine of steel and whose words were as good aspermanent. He was present in the court that day and was silent just like all the knowledgeable people there. His ethical dilemma lied between being loyal to the throne and to save a woman from being dishonoured in the court.

But, his loyalty towards the throne, should have instantly brought Draupadi in his protection. A woman has always been a symbol of 'shanthi' (peace), Lakshmi (wealth) and respect, Draupadi was the wife of the Pandavs, the daughter-in-law to the King Pandu and the 'Kul-vadhu' of the Kuru Dynasty. She was symbolic embodiment of the Respect and modesty of the Kuru dynasty. And that meant she should have been protected by the guardian of this dynasty. There was hardly anyone that could surpass Bhishma, so why didn't he do his duty?

Ethically, Bhishma should have stopped this on its very early stages but his delusion on his ethical responsibility and loyalty for the throne blinded him enough for him to become helpless at the hands of his own mind, when he had a lot more power than that.

After that comes, The Raj guru; Dronacharya another one of the prestigious member of the court and also the one that didn't utter a word during the whole cheer-haran. He was the one that taught all the various weaponry art that the pandav and the karuva learnt in their childhood. He was respected member in the court and yet he remained silent. His dilemma was very similar to the one with Bhishma, and just like in the case of Bhishma he was helpless in his own making.

Dhritarashtra, the king of Hastinapur and father of hundred kaurav brothers. Though blind, but had the strength of 100 elephants, mastered the skills of weapons but remained in silence when his son disrobed his (brother's) daughter-in-law in a court full of men. Dhritarashtra, was a wise man but someone who had religiously taken side of his sons even when they were at wrong and more often than not manipulated by his sons into something that's not right. The biggest problem with him was not his blindness of his eyes but his mind.

Even though he was king and every right to stop his sons from doing what they did, he saw the whole spectacle with sombre silence. He never asked duryodhana to stop, why didn't he? He was aware that whatever that happening in the court was absolutely wrong, his ethical dilemma lied between his blind faith in his son and his responsibility as the king to maintain the decorum of the court. It was obvious who won that fight. A king's silence towards an atrocity like this makes a huge negative statement. The man with the strength of 100 elephants but couldn't stop an open molestation of not just any women but his family's daughter-in-law.

Ethical dilemma at its worst, has brought down many great people to their knees and tied their tongue, something that was similar to a lot of people in the court that unforgettable day. I also believe that all these characters till here, paid the prices of their actions in the War itself.

Yudhishthira and the brothers had to kill people of their own family to end all the misery. Bhishma got killed by Arjun, while Shikandi stood there, Dronachrya was tricked by Yudhishthira about Ashwathama and Dhritarashtra saw all his sons die. The all paid for their karma.

Before I discuss Karn, Duryodhan and Dushasana. I would like to bring into notice a brave soul and the only person who stood up for Draupadi, Vikarana ironically he was a Kaurav. He was the only person who pointed out Draupadi, is not a property to be gambled and mistreated. Though he was shut down quickly by his other brothers, but he followed his ethics and the path to righteousness. Bhīma killed him with utter respect and out of sheer necessity as they both were opponents, but he proclaimed that Vikarana was one of the most noble warriors in the 'Kaurav Sena'.

Suryaputra Karn, the son of a Charioteer, best friend of duryodhana, illegitimate child of kunti, competitor of Arjun, 'Danraaj' Karn and there are many other aspects of this great warrior. But the aspect that I would like to look into the one that was an active participant in the Cheer-Haran of Draupadi. In the Kaurav side there were very few people that understood the concept of Dharma, one of whom was Karn himself. So why did he let this happen?

Sadly enough, Karn was not in any sort of ethical dilemma, he taunts Panchali for having five husbands and also calls her unceremonious names in a court filled with men. This seemed like a revenge for her insult during her swayamwar. But should he have that dragged it as far as calling her name and stripping her of any dignity and modesty she possessed.

It was his ethical obligation to make sure his friend is not getting to far ahead of his friends and makes blunder that could cost him his life. Karn always looked at Duryodhan as someone to whom he was obligated to show loyalty towards rather than as a friend. Which is why he never felt the need to stop what was happening in the court that day, as that would have brought questions to his loyalty and he also wanted to take revenge from Draupadi. His tactful death was a price of his Karma.

Duryodhana, the man that was the brains behind this humiliating incident. He was brilliant but a bitter man and with consistent toxic doses given by Shakuni, all he could think of how to torment the Pandav brothers and get the throne of Hastinapur. And to get that, he forgot all the boundaries ever set. The Kshatriya Dharma says not to hurt women and children during any conflict. His revenge could have ended with the brothers but, the greed of revenge blinded him. He ordered her to come into the court even when she was on her menstrual cycle. And when she doesn't agree to it, he sends Dushasana to bring her in the court. As he drags her into the court with her hair, he offers her to sit on his lap. And then orders Dushasana to disrobe her. Did he go too far with that? Was all this a revenge on her for a misplaced a laugh she had at her palace?

The conflict was between the brothers, he stripped them clean of everything he could in the game of dice. Then why did he drag Draupadi into this? He was the next-in-line for the throne or otherwise known as 'Yuvraaj', it was his responsibility his kingdom and also to take care of his family, especially the women and children, which extended to Draupadi as well seeing she was his sister-in-law. To molest a woman in the name revenge, can never be justifies or go unpunished. And he never got his hand dirty, he made his younger brother do the job for him. Which is why, he did pay for his sins by seeing all his brothers die in front of him due his own actions and got tricked in the fight with Bhīma and lost and died by his hands.

To the last character, Dushasana, the face and hands of this Molestation. Though he was religiously following orders of his elder brother, but his sins were considered just as bad his elder brother. Something to be noted here is that, when Duryodhana asks Dushasana to bring Draupadi in the court, he never asks him to slap her or drag her in with hair. This was all his personal doings. And trying to disrobe a woman, without her consent is a crime and a sin, for which paid dearly.

Draupadi washed her hair in his blood, while Bhīma drank his blood to satisfy themselves of the revenge for all the humiliation that took place that day. For the sake of the arguments, let's say that Draupadi was a slave to the Kauravs. But does that mean she loses her dignity and her right to respect in the court full of men. Should a women be molested in the court even if she is just a slave?

While looking at all the aspects that came in play, in Draupadi's Cheer-haran it is clear as a day that this was one of the darkest-days in the epic of Mahabharata. A women's dignity was robbed in the broad-day light with the presence of people from all over their kingdom and not one had the courage to stop it. It is often noticed, a women scarred always brings a battle, where not many live to tale the tale. And this event made sure that a war did take place and anyone and everyone paid the prices of their actions.

CHAPTER EIGHTEEN

REVENGE PORNOGRAPHY

Author: Manjari V, III year of B.Com LLB (Hons.) from School of Excellence in Law, Chennai.

ABSTRACT

Privacy is a myth, they say. In the current world, humans tend to crave for other's personal space. Revenge Pornography or Non – consensual discrimination means using an intimate photo or video to threaten or punish merely for the egoistic desires. It is sad truth where rape and harassment videos are searched by many and shaming people in the social media has become a new pleasure. We live in a world where sharing intimate pictures with partner has become a need to satisfy love and acceptance in most relationships. So, when they break up or get separated, one of them end up using the private photos and videos as a tool for blackmailing or threatening the other.

The 20th century didn't have many incidents in the name of revenge pornography. The revenge porn was very less in the early 2000s. The development of Internet, YouTube, Retube and porn sites were famous only after 2005. Now almost everyone owns a smartphone and internet access and the level of porn viewers increased one-third when the free internet access was given in 2016. This paper attempts to show light on the issue related to this and suggests the needed remedy to be done soon.

REVENGE PORNOGRAPHY

Revenge porn is the non – consensual distribution of sexually graphic images and videos on an online platform, it is also known as image – based sexual abuse (IBSA).[1]

Revenge pornography basically means stalking or misusing the private data. It is the upload or distribution of sexually explicit images or videos without the consent of the person in the image or video. When a person uploads another person's nudes or semi – nudes or private videos without the consent of the victim either in porn websites or in social media it is said to be revenge pornography. Technology, Social Media, Internet and lack of awareness are the main reasons for revenge pornography. We always see the fruits of the technological development and not the thorns that comes attached with the development of the same.

PORN V. REVENGE PORNOGRAPHY

The primary difference between pornography and revenge porn is the purpose of the video. Pornographic contents are recorded for various reasons either to increase the rank of the porn stars or to make profit or establish a fame and name in the porn industry whereas revenge pornography is uploaded for the reasons like insulting the victim, or making the video viral or revenge. Porn is taken and uploaded with the consent of the porn star, whereas revenge pornography is done without the consent of the victim.

On the other side, Morphing the face of the victim and placing it on a porn star's face is also done. Some people even do this out of anger or frustration of being dumped by their lover.

CASES

India's first case of revenge porn is State of West Bengal V. Animesh Boxi[2]. In this case the accused shared private images of his ex – partner without her consent because she ended the relationship with him. The victim was pressurized to share her intimate images on the pre text of marriage and later blackmailed into uploading the previous pictures to leverage more pictures from her and also to spend time with him and go outings with him. He was also accused of hacking into the phone. Being unable to take this, she ended the relationship. Later, he uploaded the intimate pictures of her in a famous website and also revealed the identity of the victim and the father.

The accused was charged under sections 354A (Sexual Harassment), 354C (Voyeurism), 354D (Stalking) and 509 (Criminal Intimidation) of the Indian Penal Code, 1860 ("IPC") and sections 66C (Identity theft), 66E (Violation of privacy) and 67/67A (Transmitting obscene material online) of the Information Technology Act 2000 ("IT Act").[3]

Accordingly, the Court found Boxi guilty of all the the offences as charged and sentenced him to five years imprisonment along with a fine of Rs. 9,000. The case is of historic significance as it is the first conviction in a 'revenge porn' case in India and the harsh punishment sends out a strong message to perpetrators of revenge pornography.

In another case of Subhranshu Rout V. The state of Odisha[4], the young man visited his classmate and raped her when she was alone at her home and also recorded this incident in his mobile. Later, the victim was threatened not to disclose this incident to anyone and if she did, the photos and videos will be leaked to the public. When the vctim opened up to her parents, he released the images and videos in Facebook using the victim's name. After police intervened, he deleted the content.The Court commented that although Rout had removed the Facebook video after the police intervention

"information in the public domain is like toothpaste, once it is out of the tube one can't get it back in and once the information is in the public domain it will never go away". He approached the court for bail. But bail was rejected as this affected a women's modesty and privacy.

Rout was charged with various offences under the Indian Penal Code, 1860 including rape (section 376), distribution of obscene content (section 292), forgery (section 465), forgery to harm reputation (section 489) and outraging a woman's modesty (section 509). Rout was also charged under the Information Technology Act, 2000 with computer-related offences (section 66), identity theft (section 66C), publishing obscenity (section 67), and publishing sexually explicit content (section 67A).

SITUATION IN INDIA

In India, Revenge Pornography has not yet been explicitly recognized as a crime and it doesn't have any specific law for it. All the cases are dealt under the broader statues of the Indian Penal Code,1860 and Information Technology Act,2000.

These offences are also covered under two sections of the Indecent Representation of Women (Prohibition) Act (IRWA), 1986.

The sections to apply will vary from case to case as the facts will be different. However, the laws relating to the breach of privacy and sexual harassment will be used.

UNDER IT ACT[5]

SECTION 66E

This section punishes the offenders with imprisonment which may extend to 3 years and a fine not exceeding 2 lakhs and in some cases both, when a person intentionally captures or publishes or transmits the intimate photographs of the victim's private body part without their permission.

SECTION 67

This section deals with the publishing or transmitting obscene and sexual material through an electronic mode, where the offender will be punished with an imprisonment up to 3 years or a fine of 5 lakhs and if the offense is committed for the second time, a term of 5 years imprisonment and with a fine up to 10 lakhs.

SECTION 67B

This section is for the children below the age of 18 years. Where any such act of publication of obscene content is made involving a child, the punishment will be imprisonment of 5 years with a fine of 10 lakh rupees.

SECTION 72

This section penalizes for breach of confidentiality and privacy.

UNDER IPC[6]

SECTION 292[7]

This section deals with the selling or distributing or letting to hire or publicly exhibiting or in any manner putting into circulation of obscene materials for which the punishment for the first conviction may extend up to 2 years and with a fine which may extend up to 2000 rupees.

SECTION 354

It explains the use of criminal force or assault on women for outraging the modesty which would impose liability for imprisonment up to 2 years or fine or in certain cases, both.

SECTION 354A[8]

According to this section, any man who advances unwelcome and sexual physical contactor asks for sexual favors, forces a woman to watch pornography or make some sexually colored remarks and statements, he will be committing sexual harassment and shall be subject to rigorous imprisonment up to 3 years or with a fine or both.

SECTION 354C

This section talks about Voyeurism, which is an act of any man who watches or captures a woman engaging in a private act, without her knowledge of being watched or filmed not expecting to be observed by the person and who shares such pictures or clips. The offender will be charged with an imprisonment of 3 years along with fine

SECTION 406

This section talks about the committing of criminal breach of trust, the offender shall be punished with an imprisonment up to 3 years with a fine or both.

SECTION 499

This section allows one to institute a suit under defamation whose criteria is whoever by words either spoken or intended to be read or by signs or by visible representations makes or publishes any imputation concerning any person intending to harm, or knowing or having reason to believe that such imputation concerning will harm, the reputation of such person.

SECTION 500

This provides punishment for person involved in defamation with a simple imprisonment for one year and may also extend to two years depending upon the case and also with fine.

SECTION 506

It provides penalty for commission of criminal intimidation where the accused will be subjected to imprisonment of 2 years or a fine or both. If the accused threatens the victim with death, grievous hurt or destruction of property or to impute unchastity of a woman shall be punished with an imprisonment up to 7 years or fine or both.

SECTION 509

This section talks about punishment for a man when he tries to insult the modesty of a woman by words, gestures, sounds or objects, intending for it to be seen or heard, intruding the privacy of the woman. Such person will be punished with imprisonment up to 1 year or fine or both.

UNDER THE IRWA[9]

SECTION 4

The victim can also file a complaint under section 4, which prohibits the act of publication or sending by post of books, pamphlets, distribution, selling, letting for hire, or circulation, etc. in the form of paper, slide, film, writing, drawing, painting, photograph, containing indecent representation of women.

SECTION 6

It provides punishment for contravening section 4 where the offender is to be punished with rigorous imprisonment and with a fine.

RISKS AND UNNECESSITY IN SENDING NUDES

There is no privacy as we think. Our lives, our thoughts, our voices and our conversations. Everything is been watched and been heard and collected. So, there is always risk employed while sharing any important information. And there is always a huger risk involved in sharing nudes.

Having access to the media and the internet, even the teens and young adults engage in sending nudes in the form of love. But where is love when there is threating to release the photos and videos of a woman for some favors or ego?

The app we use always have a copy of the photo or video in our phone and if linked to cloud storage, there will be another copy. So, when we handover the phone to family or even a repair shop, they will have access to it and might be misused.

This can lead to crimes like blackmail, cyber bullying. However, the risks don't abate even if you believe the person receiving the photos and videos wouldn't leak them. Thus, the social media is never a safe platform and we should always think twice before sending nudes as it is purely unnecessary and it involves the element of lust rather than love.

PRIVACY IS A MYTH

The conversations we think that are private are not private. It is very similar to pick up a local cordless phone over a radio scanner. Everything we say can be collected and can be used to track, stalk, steal or monitor our activity.

Privacy is definitely a myth. And they say for those who think it is not, they are just not aware. Have you ever wondered when you have searched for a random product and you get a pop up in every website that the random product is on sale? The same random product comes in the YouTube advertisements too. Its just that Google understands what we need and shows us the products. So, it is never ever safe to send any private information or private photos through internet or media. What we think that only one may see, will be seen by many.

Google CEO Sundar Pichai, once said in an interview that google stores the information. Online privacy is something which doesn't exist in reality, but made to believe that there is. All the pages we visit or surf collects data and they will use it in a way which will bring them money. Educating children once they attain a certain age of understanding all these stuffs is of ultimate necessity to avoid revenge pornography and egoistic behavior of people.

REMEDIES TO BE ADDRESSED IMMEDIATELY

When one becomes a victim of revenge pornography, one should follow the following steps.

First step is reporting to the cyber cell. They are present in every state and union territory. Upon receiving a complaint, they seize the electronic items and forward them to forensic labs to get the whole history of it. The biggest courage of the accused is anonymity and the mindset of women to speak out, that should be stricken down

Second step is to report the website or platform where you identified your image or video and send them via a legal notice to take such content.

Third step is to gather all the evidence such as chats and screenshots or call records of blackmail or threat by the accused.

The fourth step would be to file a complaint either at the national commission of women or at a local police station.

CONCLUSION

The affected victims should come out and raise complaints against such offenders as it would reduce these crimes. As of lawmakers, it is already time that a new and separate law emerges for revenge pornography to punish the offenders appropriately. The specific statute like POCSO act should be enacted to curb this menace as this is silently growing where the victims can't be identified without reporting and trough cyber cells the awareness to come out courageously with the complaints should be spread, especially to school children. When the backward mentality of speaking out about the wrong or abuse happened is a social indignity thought gets destroyed, the offenders can be immediately taken through bars of law. Along with new statute the awareness should be taken everywhere to save the future assets, our women children.

CHAPTER NINETEEN

SUPERSTITION IN INDIA: THE SOCIAL EVIL

Author: Pravesh Shekhar, M.A in Criminology and Police Studies

INTRODUCTION

It is rightly remarked, "Science is the great antidote to the poison of enthusiasm and superstition." Superstition is unquestionably ingrained in people's minds and communities worldwide. Nevertheless, in other cases, if left unchecked, a benign monster of superstition continues to feed on the gullibility of the defenceless and quickly multiplies to devour people, societies, and generations. Therefore, everyone ought to play a proactive role in finally putting an end to this atrocity.

1. A superstition is a fictitious belief, concept, or dread of something without a rational basis. It might comprise both positive and negative thoughts, ideas, and fears.

2. "Superstition" originates from the Latin word "Superstitio," which means an irrational fear of god. The English word "superstition" was derived from this Latin word.

3. Superstitions are not limited to a particular nation, religion, culture, community, area, caste, or social class; rather, they are pervasive and can be discovered in all parts of the world.

4. The practise of labelling a woman as a witch and then causing her harm, whether it be physical or psychological, is known as witch hunting. The stigmatisation of women as witches is a component of witch hunts. When a so-called "Ojha" or "Black Magician" accuses a lady of being a witch, it is common practise to incite a mob frenzy and resort to lynching as part of the legal process leading up to her execution.

5. According to the report compiled in 2021 by the National Crime Records Bureau (NCRB), human sacrifices were responsible for six

fatalities, while witchcraft was the primary factor in 68 killings.

6. The maximum number of witchcraft cases were reported from Chhattisgarh (20), followed by Madhya Pradesh (18) and Telangana (11).

7. It is extremely alarming that no central law in India specifically addresses offences involving witchcraft, Superstition, or occult-related activities.

8. The Prevention of Witch-Hunting Bill was presented to the Lok Sabha in 2016, but it ultimately failed to become law. The clauses in the proposal included punishment for charging or identifying a woman as a witch, using criminal force against a woman or torturing or humiliating a woman under the pretext of committing witchcraft.

RELEVANT PROVISIONS ON CENTRAL LEVEL

1. The Indian Penal Code (IPC) takes cognisance of human sacrifice under Section 302 (the penalty for murder), but only after the murder has been committed. Section 295A, on the other hand, attempts to discourage such practices by making them a punishable offence.

2. In accordance with Article 51A (h) of the Indian Constitution, all Indian citizens must cultivate a scientific temperament, humanism, and the spirit of inquiry and reform in their daily lives.

3. Other aspects of the Drugs and Magic Remedies Act, passed in 1954, aim to combat the crippling effects of various forms of Superstition that are common in India.

SPECIAL LOCAL LAWS ON SUPERSTITION

Only eight states in India have witch-hunting legislation so far. These include Bihar, Chhattisgarh, Jharkhand, Odisha, Rajasthan, Assam, Maharashtra and Karnataka.

1. The Prevention of Witch (Daain) Practices Act came into force in October 1999 (Bihar).

2. Jharkhand's Witchcraft Prevention Act, 2001

3. Tonahi Pratadna Nivaran Act in 2015. (Chhattisgarh)

4. Odisha Prevention of Witch-hunting Act, 2013

5. The Rajasthan Prevention Of Witch-Hunting Act, 2015

6. Maharashtra Prevention and Eradication of Human Sacrifice and Other Inhuman, Evil and Aghori Practices and Black Magic Act 2013

7. Karnataka Prevention and Eradication of Inhuman Evil Practices and Black Magic Act (2017)

8. Assam Witch Hunting (Prohibition, Prevention and Protection) Bill, 2015

CONCLUSION

It is impossible to eradicate every superstition through the passage of legislation. A conceptual shift is necessary for the elimination of these kinds of behaviours entirely, and it is something that every culture needs to adopt. Even while behaviours motivated by superstition can be extremely destructive and criminal, the law is the only institution with the authority to punish them.As a result of the country's diverse population and history, superstitions are prevalent in India. According to data from the National Crime Record Bureau (NCRB) for the year 2020, 88 people were killed for causes related to witchcraft. The state of Madhya Pradesh had the highest number of witchcraft-related killings, with 17.On the other hand, the sacrifice of human children amounted to a total of 12, with the state of Chhattisgarh with the highest number of 9.It would not be wrong to say that Witch-hunting, other crimes associated with superstition, and other superstitious behaviours that are less religious and more criminal are against the fundamental rights protected by Articles 14, 15, and 21 of the Indian Constitution. Several international laws, including the "Universal Declaration of Human Rights," the "International Covenant on Civil and Political Rights," and the "Convention on the Elimination of All Forms of Discrimination Against Women," to which India is a signatory, are also infringed by these activities.

WAY FORWARD

1. In today's day and age, the only thing that can serve as a beacon of light at the end of a dark tunnel is science and a scientific mindset. As a result, cultivating a scientific temperament and adopting central regulation are required in this millennium to restrain the evil of superstition and irrational ideas, which result in the conduct of various heinous crimes.

2. The Odisha High Court also made the observation that the state laws that are already in existence are not adequate to solve the problem, and it underlined the urgent need for a central law instead.

3. In India, legislation governing superstitions is obligatory; nevertheless, there is a prerequisite of first debating the particular elements that ought to be included. Not a single superstition can be eradicated through the power of legislation. A new point of view is necessary for this situation. Nevertheless, measures need to be taken to deal with rules that target superstitious behaviours that are exploitative, cruel and degrading.

Author's Bio

Pravesh Shekhar is a criminologist and holds a qualification from the UGC for the NET in the field of criminology itself. His master's degree in criminology and police studies was earned at the Police University in Jodhpur, Rajasthan. He finds it interesting to investigate crimes that are rooted in custom or societal norms and places an emphasis on the victims who are overlooked by the criminal justice system.

CHAPTER TWENTY

AN EXPEDITION THROUGH SACRED TO PROFANE PHASE; OF TEMPLE PROSTITUTION

Author: Malavika Anil, III year of LL.B. from CSI Institute of legal Studies , Cheruvarakonam ,Parassala, Tvm, Kerala

Co-author: Rahumath, IV year of B.Com.,LL.B. from CSI Institute of legal Studies , Cheruvarakonam ,Parassala, Tvm, Kerala

INTRODUCTION

India being a country with great varieties here exist variety of customs, rituals, traditions .one such similar tradition is the devadasi system, the literal meaning of devadasi is devas dasi or the servant of god. Its origin is said to be in the sixth century but even before that the nagarvadhu system was prominent which can be depicted from the stories of Amrapali who lived during 500 BC that is in the period of sreebuddha. The Devadasi tradition was prominent mostly in southern state like Andhra Pradesh, Karnataka, Maharashtra, Tamil nadu and in some part of Odisha. Prominence can be seen in Maharashtra, Karnataka, Andhra Pradesh and Tamil nadu .Due to cultural differences devadasi is known in different names in different parts of the country. They are called as devadasi, attakari, cottikal, tevataci, atikalmar etc. Even though they are entitled as the dasis of deva but they do have to act as mistresses for the rich, landlords, the members of royal family. They are masters of classical dance and music hence often called in palace as courtesan's .In Marathi culture there is a popular saying about devadasi that is servant of god but the wife of the whole town.

The devadasi system emerged as an impact of bhakti movement which given a spiritual status to the devdasi's. But later as the influence of the temple decreased the devadasi were considered to be as prostitute thus losing their spiritual status .As British took up the raj they treated devadasi as women's for entertainment.

POSITION OF DEVADASI'S THROUGHOUT THE AGES

This custom began during 6th century where a great queen of somavamshi dynasty decided to give an offering towards the god for showcasing her respect and to honor the almighty .The offer was nothing but a women who were wed locked to the deity and thus became the dasi of deva. As it begin for a spiritual purpose the women's who were selected as devadasi were given due respect and was treated asgoddess Lakshmi. In Andhra Pradesh there is a district called Krishna were each family in that particular area must devote one of their girl child to be devadasi's or krishnadasi's .They considered that when their girl child became devadasi the family will attain prosperity. TheCholas, Cheras, Pandya's supported the system the evidence of which can be seen the temple sculpture or their artistic work. Also in the work of KALIDASA that is Megadhutham, Malavikaangnimithram the devadasi community are been mentioned. The traveler XUAN ZANG in his writing also mentioned about the community.

From a highly respected position the devadasi's status stooped as the Mughal reign began. The influence or the importance of the temple started to decline thus the status of this community started to be cornered as mistresses or prostitute. The devadasi were once seen as an example for controlling the human instincts or as someone who controls all five senses thus controlling human natural behavior was then treated as mere opposite. Society started to discriminate this community.

When the British land up in our country and took up the gear ofrule, the condition of devadasis became worse. The British saw the devadasi's for the purpose of entertainment and they were not even given a status as a human being. Later during that period many reformist and revolutionary came up for prohibition and protection of the community. By the influence of such reformist many legislations were passed. Even though the legislations are being passed then to the conditions still remain the same.

Today in the world of development with lots and lots of legislation for prohibition and also protection of the victims of devadasi system then to there are lot and lot of cases reporting the existences of the system.

Recently the National Human Rights Commission asked the central and the state government to submit report on the measures that they have been taken for preventing devadasi system and to provide rehabilitation to the devadasi communities also the measures for restoring their social status.

The southern state especially Andhra Pradesh and Karnataka had declared the practice of devadasi system as illegal in 1982 and 1983, but then to it is stated that almost 70000 women are leading the life of devadasi's in the states. The commission which was headed by Justice Raghunath Rao found out that in Telangana and Andhra Pradesh there are around 80000 women who are still leading the life of devadasi.

The Supreme Court also has their own stand while considering the malpractice of dedicating young girls as devadasi. This system violates 'Right to life', 'Right to dignity' and also 'Right to Equality'.

CURRENT STATISTICAL CONDITIONS

For understanding the status of devadasi system in India the National Commission for Women conducted a survey in which each state which is known for the presence of this tradition should submit a report regarding the present condition, here the state of Odisha stated that there is no such reporting of devadasi's, in 2015 the last devadasi, Sasimoniwho were related to the Jaganatha temple died. Hence statistically there was no devadasi in the state of Odisha. In case of Tamil Nadu there was a total eradication of this system and currently there is no such system existing according to the records. Coming to the state of Andhra Pradesh there is almost 16,624 devadasi's in the state. In Karnataka, 2008 a survey was conducted and according to that report there was more than 40000 womens who were practicing this system, after 10 years that is in 2018 another survey was conducted and it was found that the women's practicing the system raised up to 80,000. In case of Maharashtra for providing "Devadasi maintenance allowance" application were invited and about 8793 applications were received in which 6314 were rejected due to certain defect in the application and were not eligible for the protection other 2479 applications were declared eligible. Hence it is proved that there is about 2479 women is acknowledged as devadasi and it mean that this system still persist in the state.

The National Commission for women founded that the main reasons why more and more girls are being pushed towards this system was dumbness, deafness, poverty and others.

LEGAL FRAMEWORK

The states in which the Devadasi system has its existence was predominantly in Tamil Nadu, Andhra Pradesh, Karnataka and Maharashtra, these states have enacted special legislation to tackle this situation. Many attempts have been made by Indian government to abolish the devadasi system. The initial attempt was made in 1924 by amending (Indian Penal Code, 1860) declare "the practice of dedicating girls for the ultimate purpose of engaging them in prostitution as illegal". Section 372 of IPC prohibits selling minors for the purpose of prostitution. It was prescribed that whoever disposes off person under the age of 18 years with the intent that such person shall at any age employed or used for the purpose of prostitution or illicit intercourse with any person or with knowledge that person is likely to be employed or used for any such purpose at any age is liable to prosecuted.

The preamble of the Indianconstitution states "Justice, social, economic and political; Equality of status and of opportunity; and to promote among them all Fertinity assuring the dignity of the individual and unity and integrity of the nation". Despite this there is a failure to ensure all this to devadasi's. Separate legal legislation passed by the states to curb this practice. The first effort for legislation was done by the state of Bombay in the year 1934. They enacted a new act called Bombay devadasi protection act, 1934, this act declared the practice of dedicating girls to the particular system with or without their consent as illegal.Most of the legislations have passed in southern part of India because this problem is still persistent due to large number of temples in South India. Some of the major legislation are: Madras Devadasi (Prevention of Dedication) Act of 1947, Karnataka Devadasi (Prohibition of Dedication) Act of 1988. Maharashtra Devadasi (Abolition of Dedication) Act, 2006 Juvenile Justice Act 2015 (JJ Act). The acts also provide for punishment including imprisonment of at least two years but not more than five years and fine of at least two thousand rupees but not more than five thousand rupees.

However, these laws are not strictly followed because of lack of proper implementation and awareness. Furthermore, the punishment has received criticism for being corrupt and poorly designed with reference to the degree of crime involved. It has been also noted that it's difficult to assess the accurate number of devadasi's in India.Many attempts has been made by the Supreme Court of India to implement these legislations and practices. There have been a few public interest litigations filed in the Supreme Court to examine the practice of devadasi dedications.

In Vishal Jeet v. Union of India [1990]3SCC318 the petitioner challenged the inefficiency of the police and sought for directions for implementation of the devadasi legislations and to direct the CBI to institute an enquiry against those police officers under whose jurisdiction devadasi traditions are flourishing and to take necessary action against such officers. The Supreme Court pointed that the devadasi practice is not only a social but socio-economic issue.

"A Red light trap; Society gives no chances to prostitutes off spring"

Gaurav Jain v. Union of India[1997] AIR SC 3021 the main question arose in this case was what are the rights of the children of fallen women, the modules to segregate them from their mothers and others so as to give them protection , care, and rehabilitation in the mainstream of the national life? And as a facet of it, what should be the scheme to eradicate prostitution.

The court states that the prostitutes were to be rehabilitated through self-employment schemes, and that the children should be provided adequate safety, protection and rehabilitation in the juvenile homes manned by qualified trained social workers or homes run by NGOs with financial assistance given by Government of India or State Government.

SL. Foundation v. Union of India [2014] W.P (civil) 127/2014The Supreme Court held that the direction of Dalit girls in temple in the Harappanhalli Taluk of Ballari District of Karnataka was Unconstitutional and inviolation of Article 23(1), 39(e) and (f) 14, 21 of the Indian Constitution.

DISCRIMINATION AGAINST WOMEN UNDER THE GUISE OF THE DEVADASI SYSTEM

Although the devadasi once held a revered and prominent position, with the passage of time their prominence has diminished. In the present times the practices have taken shape of prostitution. Young girls who are dedicated when they are minor are expelled out of school and deprived of their right to education. Devadasi women have no other option for income expect sexual employment and begging. They are denied the right to procreate and frequently experience sexual assault. The physical integrity of minor girls and the reproductive option open to them are crucial as they cannot to treated as commodity having no say over their bodies or as having no authority to forbid Sexual Intercourse. Devadasi's are prohibited from attending public gathering, subject to social stigma, and are forbidden from getting married even though the law holds that there is no bar to devadasi's having a valid marriage. The plight of the devadasi worsen with ages as they are unable to secure work and end up living in abject poverty.

The stigma and discrimination also extend to their children of devadasi women face discrimination at school for being illegitimate and are denied rights and privileges that accompany the status of legitimate children, such as the right to inherit. The health, education, and development of the children are seriously endangered by the societal stigma associated with illegitimate children. In particulars the daughters of Devadasi's are deprived of opportunities in education and employment and are also expected to be dedicated as Devadasis.

CONCLUSION

The system being prominent in ancient period as it had a religious masking at that time. Others give devadasi's an outlook of goddess but later as the time passed the patriarchal society showed their dominance and the community ones treated as goddess lost their social status and got a tag of prostitutes. Many legislations have been formulated for eradication and protection or rehabilitation of devadasi's and to some extend it had made impact but this system is still prevalent in certain corners of the country. They are facing many problems as the life expectancy of a child in devadasi community had dropped to fifteen. So measures must be taken not only to protect the women in the particular community but also their offspring's must be protected from the discrimination and health issues that are confronted by them.

INDIA'S UNTOUCHABLES- A BROWN SPOT IN THE RULE OF LAW

Author: Ananya Bansal, IV year of B.B.A.,LL.B. from Banasthali Vidyapith

We are the ones who started this trend of discrimination of everything. Discrimination especially occurs when individuals or groups are unfairly treated in a way and it's not just the cast or religion, it also includes freedom and speech of expression. This gap of biasness is tagging along since beginning of the humanity period, where differences began. Individuals commence the rich and poor line of status with the completion colour, propagate religion even the taxes also.

It's not just the religion and caste issues always, it sometimes appears at work places also. Youngsters are the ones who learn so easily and quickly, they have been taught the colour racism of blue and pink from very young age. The biasness of the education implies on the girl in the family. The level increases from the colour of a born child to status in the society.

WHO ARE OUTCASTS?

The humans which are not like us, the ones who are different from the society, people who are not ashamed of their body type and the citizens who are not outcasted just because they have different way of saying. The word TRANSGENDER is commonly used to say to the person who is not categorised as male or female but still that person has a heart to be known and called in the society. The recognition should be given by everybody and respectfully.

Even the supreme court of India has also said that the people of third gender should be treated equally and respectfully. There should be no biasness in the community. section 377 of Indian penal code says whoever voluntarily have sexual intercourse with the man, female or animal shall be liable in the eyes of law with the imprisonment of 10 years and fine or both. It also includes penetration to describe this offence.

After the landmark judgement case of [1]Navtej Singh Johar V/S Union of India 2018 case which states that the supreme court of India decriminalised all consensual sex among adults including homosexual sex.

WHY NAMES ARE CALLED?

The names pronounced by people to them, should be stopped as they are also the part of society. The laws have recognised them as the part of the whole community but still they are unable to fit in. making fun of their walk or gestures are not suitable to them. It moralises their confidence in this democratic community.

In the leading case of [2] National Legal Authority vs Union of India states that Discrimination on the basis of sexual orientation or gender identity includes any distinction, exclusion, restriction or preference based on sexual orientation or gender identity which has the purpose or effect of nullifying or impairing equality before the law or the equal protection of the law, or the recognition, enjoyment or exercise, on an equal basis, of all human rights and fundamental freedoms. Discrimination based on sexual orientation or gender identity may be, and commonly is, compounded by discrimination on other grounds including gender, race, age, religion, disability, health and economic status.

HOW THEY ARE SEPARATED?

The LGBTQ community represents lesbians, gay, bisexual, transgender and equal. These people are the one who are different from both the male and female gender. We are unable to accept that they areliving with the same sex gender and trying to get future ahead.

This community is not different from any other community existing in the society. The supreme court of India has given the right and passed an order for same sex marriages and even their living relationships. This is not abiding the law. The LGBTQ people faces discrimination in public places too. In 2017, during a nationwide attack on transgender people's rights. Among transgender survey respondents:

25.7 % reports say that avoiding public places such as stores and restaurants, versus 9.9 % of cisgender LGB respondents.

10.9 % reported avoiding public transportation, versus 4.1 % of cisgender LGB respondents.

11.9 percent avoided getting services they or their family needed, versus 4.4 percent of cisgender LGB respondents

26.7 percent made specific decisions about where to shop, versus 6.6 percent of cisgender LGB respondents.

These findings suggest that ongoing discrimination in public accommodations pushes transgender people out of public life, making it harder for them to access key services, use public transportation and public services or simply go to stores or restaurants without fear of discrimination.

UNEXPECTED EFFECTS

As the time passes in the working society, the major problem arises with the LGBTQ community when the major reality hits to them. While people are not accepting them as member of the community.

LGBTQ people who don't experience discrimination over work, or being fired from a job, may still find that the threat of it shapes their lives in subtle but profound ways. We question them for everything like filling the forms at any event for the preferences option or trying to humiliate them with their presence.

CONSTITUTIONAL AND LEGAL PROTECTIONS

Indian Constitution provides for positive efforts to eliminate discrimination, the Preamble to the Constitution talks about goals of achieving social, economic and political justice to everyone and to provide equality of status and of opportunity to all its citizens. Further, LGBTQ community have equal right to vote in our political system. Article 15 of the Constitution provides for prohibition of discrimination on grounds of sex also apart from other grounds such as religion, race, caste or place of birth. Article 15(3) authorizes the Sate to make any special provision for women and children. Moreover, the Directive Principles of State Policy also provides various provisions which are for the benefits of women and provides safeguards against discrimination.

In this leading case of gender discrimination [3] Neetu BalaV/S Union of India

The Constitution of India accords socio-economic and political justice, equality of status and of opportunity assuring the dignity of individual. Article 14 guarantees equality by providing that `The State shall not deny to any person equality before the law or the equal protection of the laws within the territory of India. Article 15(1) abolishes discrimination on grounds only of religion, race, caste, sex, place of birth or any of them. Article 15(2) requires that there shall be no disability, liability or restriction on grounds of sex and ensures equality of status. Article 15(3) enables the State to make special provisions for women and children. Therefore, it is expressly forbidden to discriminate on the basis of gender in cases involving public employment.

A CALL FOR ACTION

This is the high time for taking actions, if we are late now then it's never to begin with. As the time flows, we need to take these situations seriously and work upon it. The third community people should be treated with equal rights and responsibilities in the society.

To ensure that federal civil rights laws explicitly protect LGBTQ people, judiciary should pass the Equality Act, a comprehensive bill banning discrimination based on sexual orientation and gender identity in employment, public accommodations, housing, credit, and federal funding, among other provisions. Likewise, state and local governments should pass comprehensive non-discrimination protections for all. A majority power in every state and every individualin the country should support non-discrimination laws.

CONCLUSION

We the humans have tendency to make fun of disables, or untouchables or any human who is special. We never thought that is hurts someone's 's feelings but still we do that. Our law has given certain laws that same sex marriages or staying together is not illegal. It's the narrow minding thinking of humans that we can't accept the third gender in our society. Discrimination is everywhere, not just the race, caste, colour or religion. The normal ones are also facing the same discrimination at school or college for colour or may be status or anything else. After the rules and regulations, we are still lacking to accept the reality.

Author's Bio

Ananya Bansal is a law student of BBA LLB 4th year at Banasthali Vidyapith Jaipur Rajasthan. Being a law graduate, I have learnt many things which made up my mind to explore more in this new field. Well, a degree holder of law should be excellent in mooting skills but I am still learning how to be best at it. There are still my weak and strong points to be worked on and I m pretty sure that I can achieve that. Settings goals for upcoming future and deciding what's right path to choose. Learning won't make changes, trying will.

CHAPTER TWENTY-TWO

GENDER INEQUALITY IN JUDICIAL APPOINTMENTS: SHOULD WE RESERVE SEATS FOR WOMEN?

Author: Muskan Prasad, III year of B.A.,LL.B.(Hons.) from Amity Law School Noida

ABSTRACT

India is a diverse country but still, we see that number of male lawyers and judges is more in the judiciary than thefemale lawyers and this has often led us to ask questions as to why the strength of women lawyers is so less. In this paper, we will tryto discuss the causes or reasons behind gender inequality when it comes to judicial appointments and will also look into the current scenario of the representation of women and its statistics. We will also be discussing the need for gender equality in the judiciary and how it can be achieved.

INTRODUCTION

[1]India is a diverse country with diverse customs and traditions and more significantly it is a land of diverse opinions. even after having so much diversity when we try to talk about gender diversity it is seen that there is a huge gender gap which exists in every sect of the court whether it is the lower or higher court.

The fact is that since the past, India has always been a male-dominated society and has not considered or rather has not given much importance to women as a result of which women have not been allowed to play the roles that they are capable of playing in different walks of life, including the judiciary.

Though a lot has changed, and women are making their presence felt in every field, yet gender inequality prevails in every personal as well as professional sector. Gender inequality in judicial appointments is one such incident. Proper representation of women in the judicial appointment is important, it is an integral part of the government and can pave the way or remove this inequality in other fields too, but the goal seems far-fetched.

Even if everything goes as planned and [2]Justice B V Nagarathna turns out to become the first women CJI of India in the year 2027 then also this would not make much of an impact or difference as it would be about a month before she retires so practically, she won't have much time. Thus, these appointments are only symbolic and won't create much ofan impact.

Whenever a new Chief Justice takes over, they need time to settle down, the first two months are generally spent on administrative work, and with just onlya few months before retirement, she won't be able to do much of a thing. From 1950 when the Supreme court was established, it took 40 years for[3] Justice Fatima Beevi to be appointed as the first female Supreme Court judge in 1980 " I have opened the closed doors" Justice Fatima Beevi said in 2018.This had brought a positive impact but still, itwasn't much of an impact to actually change the minds of the people.

PRESENT REPRESENTATION OF WOMEN IN THE JUDICIARY

In the present scenario, the representation of women in the subordinate judiciary is less than 30% in women. Even, out of the total 25 High Court in India, 563 are male judges and 70 are women judges which constitute only 11.5%. In the Supreme Court also, the percentage of women judges is only 11% i.e., only 4 women judges and in 6 of the High Courts namely Manipur, Orissa, Meghalaya, Patna, Tripura, and Uttarakhand have no present representation of a single women judge in the High Court.

Out of 1.7 million advocates, only 15% are women and 2% are elected representatives in the state bar council are women. Through one of such data, we get to know that there is no women representative in the state bar council national committee.

REASON BEHIND THE GENDER INEQUALITY IN JUDICIARY

Indiaas a nation has been battling gender biases and prejudices since the time it gained independence. Indian judiciary does not paint a different picture. The higher judiciary's approach towards the appointment has also and always been criticized for nepotism and hypocrisy by the members of the judiciary themselves. Ever since the establishment of the Supreme

Court of India till the year 1989 all the 93 judges who have served the Apex Court have all been men. Legal education has been off-limits for women for many decades. The history has witnessed that it was only after the passing of the Legal Practitioners (Women) Act, 1923 that the bar or restriction on women for practicing law was abolished and Indian women were granted the right to take up the legal profession and practice as Advocates in the court of law. Few of them who actually made a difference by seeking legal education did not have a smooth road to walk on.

It took almost four decades after the establishment of the Supreme Court of India that, for a woman to become a judge of the Supreme Court. Practicing law has always been, identified with the men in black robes, so when women started venturing into this system, they had to identify themselves and keep up with the set of male standards that characterized a practicing advocate or judge.

Therefore, there has never been any initiative in understanding the fact as to what women can contribute to the judiciary or judicial system because they have so far always been contesting in a professional set up which was notgender-neutral. It is seen that the number of women judges in lower courts is higher than that in the higher courts

This reflects that when it comes to the selection or appointment of judges on the basis of competitive examination women judges have always proved to be better but when it comes to subjective assessment for the appointment of judges in the higher judiciary the figures are way too less. This reflects that there is no dearth of meritorious women candidates when the assessment is based on competition.

Moreover, the number of women representatives in the State Bar Council is only 2%, and in the National Bar Council its nil which needs urgent correction. Besides, there is an uncomfortable environment in the court, crowded courtrooms, lack of creches, lack of sitting places, washrooms are some of the major issues which are unfriendly to women lawyers. Among 6000 courts across the country, only 22% have separate toilets for men and women.

<u>NEED OF GENDER EQUALITY IN JUDICIARY</u>

It is a true fact in every sense that,the inclusion of women judges and lawyers will substantially improve the quality of justice delivery by giving the judiciary a diverse perspective in many ways. The higher judiciary not only is the final dispute resolution body, but it is also into determining the policies and settling up the good governance mechanism.

Presence of women in the judiciary or the judicial system symbolizes participatory democracy. Diversity of opinions gives an inclusive characteristic to the judiciary and signals equality of opportunity for all; women's participation in the judiciary will also promote equality in other areas too. Female judicial appointments especially at the senior level can shift gender stereotypes thereby bringing changes in the attitude and perception towards the appropriate roles of men and women.

This in turn can also facilitate greater representation in other decision-making positions as legislative and executive branches of the government. Gender equality in the judiciary is the need of the hour not only because it is a right for women but also because it is a right for the achievement of a more just rule of law.[4] Women judges strengthen the judiciary and help gain public trust.

Moreover, they bring those, lived experiences to their judicial actions, experiences that tend towards a more comprehensive and empathetic perspective and approach. This type of gender perspective enhances the fairness of the adjudication which ultimately benefits both men and women.

WAY FORWARD

Improving the representation of women in the judiciary is of crucial importance and have to go a long way toward a more balanced and empathetic approach in cases involving sexual violence.

For instance, in [5]an all-women bench of the Supreme Court comprising Justice R. Banumathiand Justice Indira Banerjee in State (Govt. of NCT of Delhi) vs Pankaj Chaudhary, it was held in 2018 that even if the victim was habituated to sexual intercourse, it could not be inferred that she was a "women of loose moral character" and that even if the prosecutrix was of an "easy virtue", that she has every right to refuseto submit herself to sexual intercourse.

This judgment stands in stark contrast with and ignores a 2016 all-male verdict in Raja vs State of Karnataka with a similar contrast as the above case wherein the judge had imputed an implication to the victim being " accustomed to sexual intercourse".

Changing the long-established demographics of a court can make the institution more amenable to considering itself in a new light and potentially lead to further modernization and reform. There is a must goal to achieve at least 50% representation of women in the judiciary.

There should be mandatory training for all lawyers on gender sensitization. Gender equality in the judiciary will show that the discriminatory norms against women are non-existent in the appointment of judges. A more representative gender jurisprudence would not just mean more women but in other the other hand it would increase the willingness of women to seek justice and to produce judgments that better reflect the diversity of India with experience of equal women representation in women's judiciary.

There would be a change in the judicial culture is also in a way likely to have a knock-on effect on litigants. Women's representation can bring in a new perspective and also help in bringing a positive change in the judiciary. For instance,[6] a split judgment by a division bench of the Calcutta High Court in 2015 where Justice Indira Banerjee disagreed with Justice Indrajit Chatterjee's Acquittal of a rape accused provides another example.

While Justice Chatterjee has been persuaded by the absence of external injury marks on the body of the victim, Justice Banerjee had held that "a mere act of helpless resignation in the teeth of compulsion" could not constitute consent.

In one more instance, Justice Gita Mittal was the chairperson of the committee that designed the Vulnerable Witness Project, which ensured that witnesses would not have to face the accused and could share their testimony in a comfortable and confidential space.

CONCLUSION

Advancing women's participation in the judiciary promotes the role of gender equality in a broader way thus in turn increasing the willingness of women to seek justice and also enforce their rights.

In justice women sometimes give sensitivity to the situations by looking at them from their perspective but this is not from a specific gender point of view but from a unisex point of view. It's high time that matters of gender equality in the judiciary be taken seriously and necessary steps should be taken as soon as possible.[7] As said by CJI N V Ramana that " it's a matter of right and not a matter of charity". Even Justice Nagarathna said that " female appointment particularly at the senior level can shift gender stereotypes, thereby changing attitudes and perception of appropriate roles of men and women.

SUGGESTION

This 50% reservation for women in judicial appointment is of foremost importance besides other reformation reservation would act as catalyst to cover the gender gap that prevails in our judiciary. Besides, steps should be taken to make the courts women friendly. Lawyers, judges, and other judiciary officers should be encouraged to be gender sensitive as instances of sexist remark, discrimination on the basis of gender is rampant. Educational institutes should encourage women to take up law and appear for the judiciary. The Collegium of High Court as well as the Supreme Court must encourage and make efforts to get more talented women judges in the higher judiciary for serving good many years as it would reflect party in the higher judicial system and also inculcate confidence and accelerate the justice delivery system.

By achieving gender equality in the judiciary India could become one amongst the progressive nations towards the gender parity level. Most importantly women, especially women lawyers have to remember that nobody would pave the way for them but they, have to use their inner strength and work hard to pave their path.[1] As Justice Trivedi advised women lawyers "Be a light of yourself".

CHAPTER TWENTY-THREE

THE RISING CONFLICT BETWEEN GOVERNORS AND STATE GOVERNMENT

Author: Apurv Krishna, III year of B.A.,LL.B.(Hons.) from Amity Law School, Noida.

Co-author: Shekhar Tripathi, III year of B.A.,LL.B.(Hons.) from Amity Law School, Noida.

Co-author: Suruchi Shalini, III year of B.A.,LL.B.(Hons.) from Amity Law School, Noida.

The tussle between the governors and the state government is nothing new. Ever since independence time and time again the problem has resurfaced. The governor is an important link between Centre and state. The appointment of the governor is solely in the hands of the Centre and no consultation from the state is required. The Centre also determines the tenure of the governor.

India follows the Quasi-Federal [i]structure of government, and this principle is engrained in our constitution. The Quasi-Federal structure of government in India refers to the system of government in which powers are divided between the central government and the state governments, but the central government has the power to make laws on certain subjects listed in the Constitution. The Constitution of India divides powers between the central government and the state governments in three lists: the Union List, the State List, and the Concurrent List. The Union List includes subjects on which only the central government can make laws, such as defense and foreign affairs. The State List includes subjects on which only the state governments can make laws, such as police and education. The

Concurrent List includes subjects on which both the central and state governments can make laws, such as criminal law and economic planning. The central government also has the power to make laws on subjects not listed in any of the three lists in the national interest.

But this federal structure of the government is becoming more complicated, and centre focused due to the increasing involvement of governors in the functioning of state government especially in those states where the ruling party and centre is different. Governors are being used and changed not to further constitutional goals but to further political agenda. To deal with this inconsistency in the federal structure three primary experts commissions have been formed namely Sarkaria Commission(1983) , the National Commision to Review the working of the Constitution(2000), and the Punchhi Commission(2007). These commissions dealt with many issues and suggested many changes in the structure.

Appointment of Governor

Article 153 of our constitution(PartVI) contains provisions for appointment of governor. It states that there shall be a governor for each state and one person can be appointed as governor of more than one state. It also talks about the "dual" nature of governor as the constitutional head of the state and as a representative. Article 174 of the constitution gives summoning power to the governor. It states that the governor shall from time to time summon the house or each house of the legislature of the state. Initially it was proposed that governors should be appointed on the recommendation of a sub-committee, but this was never adopted. At a later stage it was suggested that the appointment should be made from a panel but was given similar treatment.

The mode of appointment of governor was subjected to very intense debate. Leaders such as Nehru believed that someone who is not politically involved should be appointed. People who are renowned in other walks of life like education, sports, science, people from outside should be appointed.

Criticism of Governor

The role of the Governor in India has come under criticism in recent years due to the perceived degradation of the relationship between the Governor and the state government. Some of the main criticisms include:

Political bias: The Governors are appointed by the Central government, leading to allegations of political bias and partisanship. Some Governors are perceived to be working against the interests of the state government, causing tension and mistrust.

Overstepping of powers: There have been instances where Governors have overstepped their powers and taken decisions that are perceived to be beyond their purview. This has led to accusations of violation of the federal structure and infringement of the powers of the state government.

In some recent cases governors have refrained from signing the bills passed in the state assembly. Bills are sent to governors of respective states for their assent. If the governors want any changes to the bill, they can send it back with some recommendations "as soon as possible". But since this time is not defined governors are taking a long time to send it back hence withholding the bill from becoming a law. In Tamil Nadu, Governor R.N. Ravi has refrained from signing more than 20 bills in just over a year. DMK(Dravida Munnetra Kazhagam) the ruling party of the state on various occasions has accused him of acting as if he were an alternative Centre of power.

Interference in administration: Some Governors have been accused of interfering in the day-to-day administration of the state, causing resentment among the state government and the bureaucracy.

In another conflict between the governor and state government in Kerala. In a recent judgement apex court invalidated the appointment of M.S. Rajashree as Vice Chancellor of the APJ Abdul Kalam Technological University and declared it void ab initio as here hers was the only name suggested to the previous governor by the selection committee in spite of the rule that three names should be suggested. Grabbing this opportunity the governor of the state Arif Mohammed Khan ordered vice chancellor of nine other universities to hand over their resignation. Although when the ruling party put forth their concerns about the same the order was then changed to notice asking the VC to show why their appointment should not be considered void ab initio.

Lack of accountability: The Governors are not answerable to the state legislature, and this lack of accountability has led to criticism of their role and the perceived erosion of their independence.

Political appointments: The Governors are often appointed as political favours, rather than on the basis of merit. This has led to a situation where Governors are seen as political appointees, rather than impartial constitutional authorities.

Governors in recent times have become more vocal with their political views. Their support for the centre government and constant criticism of the state government is making the opposition question their neutrality. Plus the constant shift and change of governors also puts a serious question on their effectiveness and reason of appointment. In conclusion, the criticisms of the Governor in India stem from the perceived degradation of the relationship between the Governor and the state government. This has raised questions about the impartiality and independence of the Governors, and the need for reforms to enhance the role of the Governor in the Indian federal system.

Recommendations of The Punchhi Commission (2007)

The Punchhi Commission of 2007 was established to examine the functioning of the Indian Constitution and recommend changes. One of its key recommendations pertained to the role and powers of the Governor in the Indian federal system. The Commission suggested that the Governor should be seen as a representative of the President, rather than as a representative of the Centre. This would help to ensure that the Governor acts in a more impartial manner, without being influenced by the Central government.

The Commission also recommended that the Governor should be given more powers to deal with situations of constitutional crisis in the state. This would help to ensure that the Governor can take appropriate action, when necessary, without having to wait for instructions from the Centre. The Commission also recommended that the Governor should have the power to dismiss the state government in cases of constitutional breakdown or when the government is acting in a manner that is harmful to the interests of the state.

The Punchhi Commission also recommended that the Governor should have the power to appoint the Chief Minister in case of a hung assembly, where no party has a clear majority. This would help to ensure that the Governor can play a more active role in the formation of a government, and that a stable government is formed in a timely manner.

In conclusion, the Punchhi Commission's recommendations regarding the role of the Governor in the Indian federal system are aimed at enhancing the Governor's role as an impartial constitutional authority, while giving them more powers to deal with situations of constitutional crisis in the state. These recommendations are aimed at strengthening the Indian federal system and ensuring that the interests of the state are protected.

CASES

In India, the Supreme Court has issued several judgements regarding conflicts between the Governor and the state government. These judgements have established the powers and responsibilities of the Governor, as well as the limits of those powers.

Now, even the Supreme Court has dealt with this issue many times. In its judgment in Shamsher Singh vs State of Punjab (1974), [ii]one of the most influential decision relating to this matter Supreme Court held that the president and the governor in terms of power are nothing more than a constitutional head in a cabinet type of government. Although there are few exceptions to this rule. Now these exceptions are more evident in the case of the governor hence the conflict arises from time to time.

In the case of S. R. Bommai v. Union of India (1994), [iii]the Supreme Court held that the Governor's power to dismiss a state government is subject to judicial review. The Court also established that the President's power to impose President's rule (Article 356) in a state can only be invoked in certain exceptional circumstances, such as a breakdown of constitutional machinery in the state.

In the case of B. P. Singhal v. Union of India [iv](2010), the Supreme Court held that the Governor must act on the advice of the Council of Ministers, except in certain exceptional circumstances, such as when there is a constitutional crisis.

In the case of Rameshwar Prasad v. Union of India (2006)[v], the Supreme Court held that the President's power to dissolve a state assembly and call for fresh elections is subject to judicial review.

In the case of R. K. Garg v. Union of India (1981)[vi], the Supreme Court held that the Governor's power to reserve a bill for the President's assent is not absolute and can be challenged in court.

In conclusion, the Supreme Court of India has established that the Governor's powers are not absolute and are subject to judicial review and that the Governor must act on the advice of the Council of Ministers in most circumstances.

Conclusion

The role of governor is very important in maintaining a healthy relation between state and centre. But the same cannot be achieved when he is being used as a tool to further political objectives. Some changes need to be made to the appointment process and who can be appointed. Deriving from the idea of Nehru[vii], a governor should be someone who is an eminent personality in some field. It is also very important that he should not be politically connected or active. He should be from outside the state to maintain a fair relation. In addition to all this the appointment should be after consultation with the state government. Individuals who occupy higher posts in judiciary like judges should not be allowed to be appointed as governors after retirement.The discretionary power of the governor also needs to be defined for further clarification. Constitutional amendments regarding all these needs to be made for proper and effective implementation.

www.ingramcontent.com/pod-product-compliance
Lightning Source LLC
Chambersburg PA
CBHW072237150726
48002CB00005B/2129